A spectacular chocolate Shar-Pei. Dar Mon's Chocolate Mousse. Owner: Kathi Mann. Margery Denton, photo.

THE CHINESE SHAR-PEI
VETERINARY MANUAL
by
Kelly Anne Tate, R.N.
and
Jay Jakubowski, D.V.M.

Medea Publishing Company Inc.
P.O. Box 3589
Washington, D.C.

Library of Congress Cataloging in Publication Data

Tate, Kelly Anne; Jakubowski, Jay D.V.M.
  The Chinese Shar-Pei Veterinary Manual

  Bibliography: p. 000
  Includes Index
  1. Chinese Shar-Pei Veterinary Manual   I. Tate and Jakubowski
II. Title

LOC 85-063574
ISBN 0-911039-06-6

Editor: Paul Strang
Assistant Editor: Maureen Dwyer
Manuscript and Production Editor: Kelly Tate
Illustrative and Graphic Design: Karen O'Neil
Photographer: Rear Cover, Margery Denton
Illustrator: Marilee Carroll
Front Cover, Peter Schweitzer

International Standard Book Number: 0-911039-06-6
Library of Congress Catalog Card Number: 85-063574

Acknowledgements

This book is made possible through the overwhelming support and information offered by hundreds of Shar-Pei breeders and veterinarians around the country. Without their concern and generosity, this effort would not have been possible.

Special thanks are in order to those breeders who shared with us their knowledge and concerns, victories and failures, joys and heartaches and, above all, their pride in the Shar-Pei and hopes for the future of the breed. Their love, honesty and devotion are evident in the selfless time and effort required to track down what was sometimes obscure information. It is our fervent wish that our work will help to clarify and illuminate some of the more common, but nonetheless complex, problems of the Shar-Pei.

Thanks are also in order for the numerous veterinarians who contributed their technical and theoretical expertise. Whether it was a highly sophisticated university research laboratory or a one-vet clinic, their advice, experience, and suggestions were invaluable.

We would like to extend our heartfelt gratitude to some very special people: Betsy Davison, current breeder, Shar-Pei author, and former editor of *The Golden Dragon Newsletter*. Betsy's histories, records and photographs kept our goals and ambitions in sight. And a special thanks also goes to Margery Denton, whose photographic skills leave us awed.

Our deepest appreciation goes to our literary personnel: Dr. Terrence Earls, who kept our "i's" dotted and our "t's" crossed; and to Dr. Louise Kehoe, whose enthusiastic support kept us going when the magnitude of the task threatened to engulf us. And perhaps most important, a heartfelt thank you to Thomas Tate, Kelly's husband, who had the conviction, love, and above all, patience to believe in the importance of this project.

Our wish is that this book and its information be used for the Shar-Pei's best of health.

Sincerely,

Dr. Jay Jakubowski
Kelly Anne Tate, R.N.

CONTENTS

Acknowledgments

Chapters

CHAPTER ONE

INTRODUCTION TO THE CHINESE SHAR-PEI

Nothing in Nature is perfect. Whether it is man or beast, there is always some degree of "poetic license" taken with the physical creation. The imperfection may be structural or within a functioning system. It may be glaringly obvious or more subtle and discrete, but it is present nonetheless. The amazing part is that, in spite of flaws, a being is able to exist, function, and in most cases even flourish.

Some species seem to have certain

physical areas which are more vulnerable, more prone to disorder. In the racehorse it is the legs and lungs; in the male cat it is the urinary tract; in man it is many areas, ranging from the lowly knee to the mighty heart. It is not a question of whether, but of where or what.

In the canine family, tendencies for disorder also exist. In certain breeds the areas are well defined, occurring so often that the method of treatment has become traditional and routine. The Scottish Terrier's skin problems, the German Shepherd's hips, the Dachshund's back, and the Collie's eyes have all been recognized as weak points in the physical construction of those specific breeds. This does not mean that these breeds are of any less quality, but merely that those specific physical areas have a higher than usual susceptibility to dysfunction. Just as a 45 year old man suffering from heart disease is not "at fault" for his medical condition, so, too, these dogs are not at fault for their physical weaknesses.

Just as a man does not contract every disease, a dog breed is not prone to every disease. In the Shar-Pei, there do exist a handful of disorders that recur within the breed as a whole. It must be remembered, however, that not every Shar-Pei develops these conditions. The health of each individual dog is particular to his own genetic roadmap.

Since the political revolution in the Chinese homeland of the Shar-Pei, private ownership of dogs is severely discouraged. Viewed in China as a symbol of decadence, dogs are seen as wasteful of scarce food and medical resources. Thus, the Shar-Pei arrived in America with a history that is clouded by small remaining numbers, political persecutions, language and cultural barriers. Only as the years have passed have American breeders been able to determine, by experience, what medical conditions relate to the Shar-Pei. For many practitioners some of these disorders have rarely been seen. As a result, the Shar-Pei began to develop a reputation for having exotic and complicated medical tendencies that were somehow different from those of "regular" dogs.

What this book attempts to do is to show that the vast majority of the particular afflictions to which the Shar-Pei is subject are neither exotic nor insurmountable. They are merely new constellations of conditions occurring in a breed that is, in itself, rare. Each medical condition, when approached logically and professionally, can be seen to be the very same condition that can appear even in the unpretentious cross-breed. It is the breed of dog that is rare and unusual, not the quality of medical problems that occur within that breed!

Unfortunately for many frustrated owners, the Shar-Pei's "wrappings" have served to cloud his true medical characteristics. This is not to underestimate the challenge that some of these "common" health problems can engender. In any animal, large or small, rare or commonplace, the presence of a physical malady will inevitably complicate its ownership.

It is our fervent hope that this text will shed some light on the quality and quantity of those specific disorders that can affect the Shar-Pei. We hope that it will dispel some of the myths and misinformation that plague the reputation of this fine breed. We hope that this medical information will be of value to owner and breeder alike. Above all, we hope that if in fact a rare and exotic medical condition is actually identified, the public spirit will be one of research, education, and cooperation.

THE CHINESE SHAR-PEI

Three beautiful, healthy Shar-Pei puppies. Wrinklee Loves Ching Tu X Kellair's Shadowfax puppies. Margery Denton, photo.

There are some animals that, when you look deeply into their eyes, you realize that the animal is looking back with similar depth and intensity. It can be a very disconcerting experience! That level of intelligence and acute awareness is clearly evident in the eyes of the Shar-Pei. He is a thinking dog, active and alert, fully confident that equal is viewing equal.

The Shar-Pei is a surprising dog in many ways. His enchanting puppyhood, full of wrinkles and folds, makes him one of the most unique members of the dog world. As an adult, the pup's baggy, over-sized costume becomes a well-tailored suit, appropriate for this calm and dignified animal. The transformation from charming to classy is part of the mystery that surrounds this breed.

Ch. Tai-Pan's Odie of Kasu, C.D. at two years. Note the proud stance of the Shar-Pei. Kasu Kennels.

Showlines Papani of Jewel at six weeks. Robin Cimock, breeder. Jennifer Jewell, owner.

Originally bred for fighting, the Shar-Pei required stamina, agility, intelligence and courage. If a dog failed to succeed in his role, he was unceremoniously destroyed. This practical, calculated approach, though repugnant to Americans, did serve to cull the weak and undesirable animals from the breed. Although he is no longer used for fighting, those same qualities that once served him in the combat ring are still valued in everyday life. Loyalty, perseverance and bravery make the Shar-Pei a valuable family companion and guardian.

Nearly lost to extinction by Chinese politics in the 1950's, the breed was kept alive by a few devotees in South China, Macao and Hong Kong. In 1971 an American magazine ran a photograph of a Shar-Pei, indicating that he was one of the last remaining examples of the breed. This initiated the attempt of a few Hong Kong dog breeders to re-establish the Shar-Pei. In 1973 another magazine article and photograph triggered such a positive American response that a few members of the breed soon obtained residency on this side of the ocean. Today there are approximately 20,000 Shar-Pei thriving under the loving care of American owners. The same physical charm and even temperament that intrigued Americans 16 years ago is still present in the breed today.

There is a composed, gentle, almost

Ch. Chesapeake's Creme D'Caspar at ten weeks. Jill Parslow, breeder/owner.

cat-like quality to the typical Shar-Pei. The adult seems to carry himself with the dignity of a breed that has seen the passing of ages. His quiet devotion, cleanliness and sensitivity endear him to his human companions. Good with children, he is protective yet fun-loving. His grooming needs are minimal; he strives to learn proper indoor etiquette at a young age. If properly socialized as a puppy, his love of people makes him his own best ambassador.

The Shar-Pei can be a source of joy and pride for the family that challenges his mind, encourages his obedience, and nourishes his emotional needs. His breeding history should always be remembered however, for underneath the charm is a powerful animal. Although only medium-sized, there still lingers the assertiveness and bravado that ensured his survival in less "civilized" environments.

As the Shar-Pei continues to flourish, breeders are striving to produce quality animals that will continue this heritage. As in any breed, selection of a new puppy requires much thought and investigation. In the Shar-Pei, due to his relative rarity, a buyer can expect to spend anywhere from a few hundred dollars to thousands depending on the quality of the dog. However, the pur-

Ling Ling's Bad to the Bone at five months and friend, Heaven Smith.

chase of a Shar-Pei should be for the joy of his companionship, not merely the acquisition of a novelty.

The recurring recommendation from breeders throughout the country was for a buyer to take his time! Researching the local breeders, going to shows to see a number of dogs, and thinking carefully about the selection of a specific puppy are all strongly encouraged. The prospective owner must be realistic about his ability not only to afford a good quality dog, but to be able to abundantly provide for his physical, emotional and training needs. Above all, regardless of the breed's new-found American popularity, the dog must ultimately be happy in the home and the home happy with the dog.

Whenever dealing with a rare breed, accurate information is typically scarce

Ho Wun II Scherzando at two years. Nancy Mellema, owner.

Five week old pups learning about stairs. Helen Armacost, breeder.

or difficult to obtain. The following newsletters and clubs are highly recommended resources for the potential buyer:

- The Chinese Shar-Pei Club of America 55 Oak Court, Danville, CA. 94526 (They can furnish addresses of local clubs; they also publish an official Shar-Pei publication called *The Barker*.)
- *The Golden Dragon Newsletter* Milessa Mullinax, P.O.Box 71974 Marietta, GA. 30007
- *The Orient Express II Newsletter* Jo Ann Redditt, P.O. Box 6468 Arlington, Va. 22206
- *The Pelican Newsletter* Betsy Davison, editor 1009 23rd Street, Sarasota Florida, 33580

There are also a few good books on the breed that cover the history, purchasing, and other vital information about the Shar-Pei breed.
- *The Chinese Shar-Pei* by Eve Olsen and Paul Strang It can be obtained from Denlinger's Publishers, LTD. Box 76, Fairfax, Virginia 22030

- *The Chinese Shar-Pei Puppy Book* by Jo Ann Redditt
  It can be obtained from Medea Publishing Company LTD., P.O. Box 3589, Washington, D.C. 20007
- Medea Publishing will be releasing another book on the Shar-Pei in 1988 which will deal with puppy and dam care—from mating through caring for the new puppy.

Breeders may also be located in the Classified Section of the *Dog World* and *Dog Fancy* Magazines.

OFFICIAL STANDARD OF THE CHINESE SHAR-PEI IN AMERICA
effective January 1, 1988

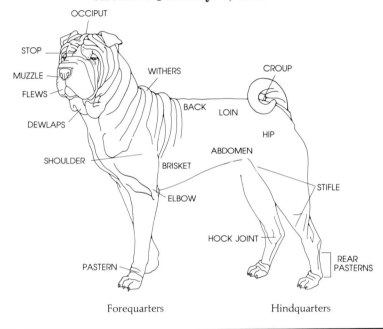

Forequarters   Hindquarters

As approved by the Chinese Shar-Pei Club of America, Inc., courtesy of Betsy Davison.

General Appearance

An alert, dignified, active, compact dog of medium size and substance, square in profile, close coupled, the well proportioned head slightly but not overly large for the body. The short harsh coat, the loose skin covering the head and the body, the small ears, the "hippopotamus" muzzle shape and the high set tail impart to the Shar-Pei a unique look peculiar to him alone. The loose skin and wrinkles covering the head, neck and body are superabundant in puppies but these features may be limited to the head, neck and withers in the adult.

Head

Large, slightly but not overly, proudly carried and covered with profuse wrinkles on the forehead continuing into side wrinkles framing the face. Skull—Flat and broad, the stop moderately defined, the length from nose to stop is approximately the same as from stop to occiput. Muzzle—One of the distinctive features of the breed. It is broad and full with no suggestion of snipiness. The lips and top of muzzle are well padded and may cause a slight bulge at the base of the

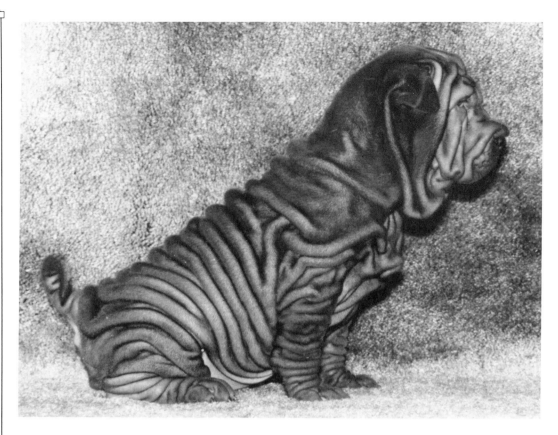

Chi-Kuan's Rufflestuff at five weeks. Maryellen Arnold, owner.

nose. Nose—Large and wide and darkly pigmented, preferably black but any color nose conforming to the general coat color of the dog is acceptable. In dilute colors, the preferred nose is self-colored. Darkly pigmented cream Shar-Pei may have some light pigment either in the center of their noses or on their entire nose. Teeth—Strong, meeting in a scissors bite. Deviation from a scissor bite is a major fault. Eyes—Dark, small, almond-shaped and sunken, displaying a scowling expression. In the dilute colored dogs the eye color may be lighter. Ears—Extremely small, rather thick, equilateral triangles in shape, slightly rounded at the tips, edges of the ear may curl. Ears lie flat against the head, are set wide apart and forward on the skull, pointing toward the eyes. The ears have the ability to move. Prick ears are

a disqualification. Tongue, Roof of Mouth, Gums and Flews—Solid bluish-black is preferred in all coat colors except in dilute colors, which have a solid lavender pigmentation. A spotted tongue is a major fault. A solid pink tongue is a disqualification. (Tongue colors may lighten due to heat stress; care must be taken not to confuse dilute pigmentation with a pink tongue.)

Body

Proportion: The height of the Shar-Pei from the ground to the withers is approximately equal to the length from the point of breastbone to the point of rump. Neck—Medium length, full and set well into the shoulders. There are moderate to heavy folds of loose skin and abundant dewlap about the neck and throat. Back—Short and close-coupled, the topline dips slightly behind the withers, slightly rising over the short, broad loin. Chest—Broad and deep with the brisket extending to the elbow and rising slightly under the loin. Croup—Flat, with the base of the tail set extremely high, clearly exposing an up-tilted anus. Tail—The high set tail is a characteristic feature of the Shar-Pei. The tail is thick and round at the base, tapering to a fine point and curling over or to either side of the back. The absence of a complete tail is a disqualification.

Forequarters

Shoulders—Muscular, well laid back and sloping. Forelegs—When viewed from the front, straight, moderately spaced, with elbows close to the body. When viewed from the side, the forelegs are straight, the pasterns strong and flexible. The bone is substantial but never heavy and is of moderate length. Feet—Moderate in size, compact and firmly set, not splayed. Removal of front dewclaws is optional.

Hindquarters

Muscular, strong, and moderately angulated. The metatarsi (hocks) are short, perpendicular to the ground and parallel to each other when viewed from the rear. Hind dewclaws must be removed.

Ch. Chesapeake's Creme d'Caspar all grown up at two years.

Champion White Dragon Abracadabra Mo Shu. Lucky Wun Kennels.

Coat

The extremely harsh coat is one of the distinguishing features of the breed. The coat is absolutely straight and off-standing on the main trunk of the body but generally lies somewhat flatter on the limbs. The coat appears healthy without being shiny or lustrous. Acceptable coat lengths may range from the extremely short ''horse coat'' up to the ''brush coat'', not to exceed one inch in length at the withers or a coat that has been trimmed is a major fault. The Shar-Pei is shown in its natural state.

Color

Only solid colors are acceptable. A solid colored dog may have shading, primarily darker down the back and on the ears. The shading must be variations of the same body color (except in sables) and may include darker hairs throughout the coat. The following colors are a disqualifying fault: Albino, Brindle, Particolor (patches), Spotted (spots, ticked, roaning), and a tan-pointed pattern (typical black and tan or saddled).

Gait

The movement of the Shar-Pei is to be judged at a trot. The gait is free and balanced with the rear feet tending to

Chi-Kuan's Off With'a Bang at eight weeks. Five time "Best Puppy" winner before four months of age. Ellana Clarke, owner/breeder.

converge on a center line of gravity when the dog moves at a vigorous trot. The gait combines good forward reach and a strong drive in the hindquarters. Proper movement is essential.

Size

The preferred height is 18 to 20 inches at the withers. Average weight is 40 to 55 pounds. The dog is usually larger and more square bodied than the bitch but both appear well proportioned.

Temperament

Regal, alert, intelligent, dignified, lordly, scowling, sober and snobbish, essentially independent and somewhat standoffish with strangers, but extreme in his devotion to his family. The Shar-Pei stands firmly on the ground with a calm, confidant stature.

Major Faults:

1. Deviation from a scissors bite
2. Spotted tongue

Weena and Lola. Note the strong, sound bodies. June Collins, owner/breeder.

Left: Ch. Xanadu General Issi-Mo. Right: Ch. Genaul Megan Xanadu, C.D. Only Shar-Pei bitch ever to win Baltimore's prestigious International Show in 1985. Won Best of Breed over 142 Shar-Pei entries. Helen Armacost, owner.

3. A soft coat, a wavy coat, a coat in excess of 1″ in length at the withers or a coat that has been trimmed.

Disqualifying Faults:

1. Pricked ears
2. Solid Pink tongue

3. absence of a complete tail

4. Not a solid color, i.e.: Albino; Brindle; Parti-colored (patches); Spotted (including spots, ticked or roaning); Tan-pointed pattern (including typical black and tan or saddled patterns)

Note the "prick" ears, an inherited trait.

CHAPTER TWO

OPTHALMIC DISORDERS

CORNEAL ULCERATION

The clear, smooth covering of the anterior one-sixth of the eyeball is called the cornea. It is directly continuous with the sclera which slightly overlaps it. The cornea is made up of fibrous tissue yet it has no color and, in the healthy eye, is completely transparent. The cornea has been called "the window of the eye." Through this clear cornea can be seen the colored iris and the dark pupil. The integrity and the clarity of the cornea greatly affect the quality of vision; even if all the other structures of the eye are intact, if the cornea is damaged or scarred, vision will be compromised.

The cornea's surface layer is a thin sheath of epithelial cells. Most injuries or diseases begin by adversely changing the cornea at the epithelial level. Once these cells have been damaged, in essence the integrity of the eye has been breached.

Inflammation of the cornea is called keratitis. If it also involves loss of tissue, it is classified as a corneal ulceration. The offending agent may be a foreign body, a microorganism such as a bacteria, a virus, a fungus, or an injury from an entropic hair. Inflammation, called anterior uveitis, can spread deeper into the anterior chamber causing surrounding structures such as the iris to inflame. (See Anterior Uveitis) In severe cases gravity may cause pus to settle at the bottom of the cornea, thereby giving it a yellowish-white appearance.

Any ulceration or injury to the cornea must be considered a serious condition. The healing of all but the smallest of injuries may result in a decrease of vision. If there is ever any question, the owner should not hesitate to seek veterinary assistance. Cornea problems do not respond to home remedies.

Corneal injuries are very painful. The white sclera of the eye may appear "bloodshot." The dog will typically display signs of discomfort: squinting, tearing of one or both eyes, pawing at the eye or rubbing it against objects, and photophobia. In an attempt to assist

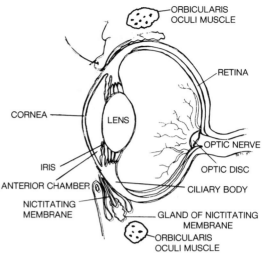

The inner structure of the normal canine eye.

in the healing process, tiny blood vessels will grow into the clear cornea. These blood vessels add to the distortion of vision. The area immediately surrounding the ulcer may have a diffuse cloudy appearance due to being swollen with fluid. As the condition worsens, the eye becomes susceptible to more extensive damage. Small "craters" can erode down into the deeper tissues. If the condition is not treated, the ulceration may invade so deeply that the iris actually collapses into the resulting "hole," an ominous condition called iris bombay.

Large ulcerations caused by foreign bodies or delayed medical treatment may be seen by the naked eye. To the owner they may appear as dull spots on the surface of the eye. Smaller ulcers can be visualized only after staining the cornea with fluorescein. This solution will not adhere to a normal cornea. If there is an area that is injured or ulcerated, the stain will cling and be visible under magnification. The staining process is painless and extremely accurate. In a matter of minutes, the vet can pin-

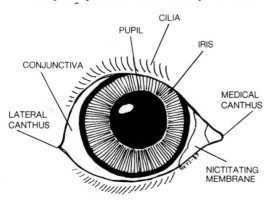

The normal canine eye.

point the area of concern and begin to discern why that area has been injured.

Early treatment is very important in cornea injuries. If left to go untreated for even three to four days, the cornea may try to heal itself. Unfortunately, this healing process is usually faulty, leaving an "indolent border." The edges of this border can never mesh properly.

If the ulcer is extensive or incorrectly healed, a procedure called "debridement" may be necessary. The vet will first instill an anesthetic solution to numb the eye's surface, then he will take a sterile Q-Tip and gently scrape the edges of the ulcer. This procedure will clean away old, injured cells. The new layer of eye cells will then have a chance to neatly heal.

Treatment of ulcerations follows a two step-pattern: first, antibiotic eye medications alone will be instilled until the lesion is healed. During this first stage of healing, while the pain decreases, it is possible for other symptoms to become worse: the edema may increase as may the small blood vessels within the cornea. If edema and/or blood vessels persist, then combination antibiotic/steroid eye ointments will be the following step. This second stage minimizes the possible scar formation in the cornea. Throughout the treatment, systemic antibiotics may be required.

With severe eye disease, the dog should be kept quiet in a darkened room. Any drainage from the eye should be gently washed away with warm sterile water three or four times a day. Eye ointments should be instilled as directed by the vet. Warm compresses held gently to the eye can help to relieve the pain of this condition.

Approximately one to four weeks are required to heal a corneal ulceration. Most vets will re-stain the eye every three to five days to assess the healing process. If healing does not occur in four weeks, a more extensive surgical repair may be necessary.

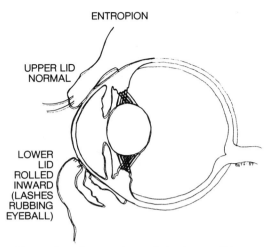

Example of entropion of the lower lid.

Prompt treatment of the condition may prevent extensive eye compromise. If the condition is caught in time, and treatment is aggressive, the prognosis is excellent.

ENTROPION

Entropion, or the rolling of the eyelid inward against the eyeball, is a common congenital defect within many breeds. The Irish Setter, Golden Retriever, Chesapeake Bay Retriever, Great Dane, Great Pyrenees, Saint Bernard, Kerry Blue Terrier, Norwegian Elkhound and Bulldog all are subject to entropion. However, breeds that have abundant facial and head skin, such as the Chow, Shar-Pei, and Bloodhound are especially prone to this condition. Entropion is also found in the horse, sheep and cat. Although entropion is suspected of being an inherited trait, the means of inheritance is still unknown. Most breeders of affected dogs are diligently searching for a way to eliminate this characteristic.

In the Shar-Pei puppy the excessive skin of the head is one of the factors that allows the eyelids to roll inward. The resulting corneal irritation is not only painful, but it can cause serious damage to the cornea. Entropion in these puppies may be apparent soon after they open their eyes, at approximately 10-

14 days. Severely affected Shar-Pei puppies are typically brought to the vet in the second to third week of age.

The degree of entropion is the major determination for treatment. If the animal is in pain, even at as young as four weeks of age, or there is ocular damage, the practitioner will take steps to correct the condition. Left untreated, entropion can cause permanent corneal scarring. Treatment for entropion depends on the severity of the condition and the age of the animal. The approach for a four week old puppy may be entirely different from the treatment for a year old dog. The deciding factor is the amount of damage being done and the discomfort of the animal. Obviously, most practitioners will not hold off treatment if the animal's health is being affected.

Entropion is classified as a congenital, spastic or acquired disease. It may affect the upper lid only or both upper and lower lid; one eye may be involved or both. In congenital entropion the extent of the problem may involve as little as one area on one eye or it may be so severe as to involve the entire lid. However, the location of the eyelid's inward roll does not seem to have a connection to the severity of the problem. The end result is the same: the dog is in obvious discomfort.

Spastic entropion occurs when the orbicularis oculi muscle goes into a painful spasm. The condition occurs most often when other chronic conditions are present, such as a corneal ulcer or trauma, uveitis or some eyelid diseases. Treatment of the underlying medical problem may alleviate the situation; at times, however, surgical intervention may be required. Spastic entropion is usually confined to a single eye.

Acquired entropion is developed secondary to trauma, foreign bodies, tumors, surgery or chronic irritation. It is usually confined to one eye.

To further complicate matters, a dog's condition can be caused by more than one type of entropion. A dog may have congenital entropion as well as spastic entropion. The vet must determine which type(s) of entropion affects the dog and base the treatment on those findings. Many parts of the country have ophthalmologists who specialize in the treatment, both medical and surgical, of the eye and surrounding tissues.

The symptoms of entropion are directly related to the amount of involvement of the eyelid. Just as in any disease there are levels of severity: with a minor cold, an aspirin may handle the symptoms; but with pneumonia, antibiotics are required. So with entropion, the symptoms relate to exactly how much of the lid rolls inward and how that individual dog reacts to the irritation. Some practitioners feel that the physical characteristics of the eyelid hairs themselves, their stiffness and their number, have a direct relation to how a specific dog will react.

The owner may observe a number of signs that the dog is suffering from eye irritation: rubbing the face either with the paw or along the floor, an eye discharge that can be either clear or yellow, or blepharospasm (squinting). It may begin suddenly or gradually depending on the underlying cause. In any case, the owner will usually not be able to see the offending hairs on the eyeball. A veterinarian will be able to readily diagnose the problem by using an ophthalmoscope.

The vet's job is to confirm the presence of entropion, evaluate the degree of involvement and decide on the best course of action. It will be necessary to examine the cornea in order to determine the amount of irritation or damage. Smaller ulcers can be visualized only after staining the cornea. This is done by gently instilling fluorescein, a staining solution, into the eye. This staining fluid will outline the exact location and size of any ulcers. A close look under magnification will usually show the offending eyelid hairs actually rubbing against the eyeball with every blink, every movement of the eye itself.

Depending on the area of the country, the exposure to the disease that the practitioner has had, and the wishes of the owner, treatment may encompass the use of ointments to ease the irritation to full blown, highly technical surgical procedures. Entropion treatment is not a one-method-fits-all approach. The latest data on entropion shows that treatment is divided now into two levels: initial, used for the very young pup; and permanent, used for the mature dog or more severe cases.

Initial treatments are typically employed when the animal presents with the condition as young as four weeks of age. Most vets are uncomfortable doing a more permanent procedure, especially on the Shar-Pei, when the animal has not matured into its full size and structure. The Shar-Pei goes through such marked facial and head changes as it matures that skin which did not

Tacking for entropion.

"fit" in its puppyhood may well be perfect as an adult. If, however, there is overt ocular damage occurring even at a few weeks of age, most specialists state that they would perform a more permanent repair to prevent long term eye scarring.

Basically, the initial treatments are used to stall for time. Time gives the pup a chance to "grow out of it." The first treatment may be in the form of ointments which lubricate the contact points between the eyeball and the eyelid. Ointments must be applied regularly and religiously in order to be effective, often as frequently as every two hours. It takes a strong commitment on the part of the owner to follow this regimen.

Another initial treatment is a semi-surgical technique called "tacking." Tacking has been used for years in the treatment of sheep and horses but has only in the past few years been tried in the dog. It is based on the concept that if the eyelid can be moved away from the cornea, the eye will heal and give the animal time, hopefully, to grow out of it. In traditional tacking methods, sutures are placed through the offending upper or lower area of eyelid. The eyelid

An alternate method of eyelid tacking using short pieces of plastic tubing to prevent sutures from pulling through the skin.

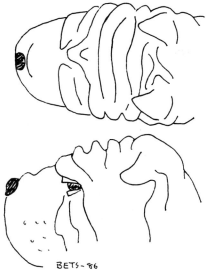

Four weeks old pups with head-tacks secured by shirt buttons.

Head tacking for entropion. Courtesy of Betsy Davison.

is fan-folded back onto itself, thereby being pulled up and away from the cornea. The sutures are tied and left in place. The animal is still able to blink and close his eyes, but the exterior margin of the lid is no longer rubbing against the eyeball.

A newer approach to entropion tacking involves the suturing together of various facial wrinkles instead of the eyelid tissue. By using the thicker skin of the cheek and forehead, the vet is able to pull up enough skin that the eyelids are shifted back from the cornea. This type of head tuck can be strategically placed to treat both upper or lower lid entropion as needed.

Most vets are currently using a thin nylon suture material that is strong and dependable. It does not seem to cause the small areas of inflammation and scarring at the suture's entry and exit sites as does a silk suture material. Unless the dog responds severely, any minor tacking scars will be temporary, fading in approximately three to four months.

Sutures, unfortunately, do not stay in place forever. The tissue of a young pup's eyelids is especially fragile. In many cases the sutures will begin to tear through the skin. If the sutures remain in place for three to four weeks, the procedure is considered successful. Some practitioners have resorted to using men's plastic, two-hole shirt buttons on the top side of the suture stitch to prevent them from sawing through the eyelid or facial tissue. The buttons provide a greater surface area, allowing the pressure of the sutures to be more widely distributed. Regardless, repeated tacking may be required in order to give the dog time to mature. For this reason, if the condition is severe, many practitioners will elect to perform a more permanent correction rather than subject the dog to multiple tacking procedures.

Pre-operative care begins at home. The owner begins by following the instructions given to them by the vet. While each vet hospital will have its own special requests and rules, the general approach is to keep the dog without food for eight to sixteen hours prior to the surgery as most vets use general anesthesia for the tacking procedure. Although some vets have begun to use minimal sedation for the procedure, food and water would still be withheld. The withholding of food and fluids helps to prevent the dog from inhaling these should he vomit during or after the operation; pneumonia or suffocation are possible consequences of the breathing-in of vomitus.

Post-operative care involves watching that the dog recovers completely from the anesthetic. The dog should be aware of his surroundings, although he may still be groggy. The owner should provide a warm, draft-free, quiet place for him to recover. He should be allowed to relieve himself outside, while leashed, every six to eight hours. Water may be offered when he is fully alert and food may be offered once he is able to walk normally.

The immediate post-op eye will look swollen and uncomfortable for approximately three to five days. This is the tissues' normal reaction to the surgery and does not mean that anything is amiss. The physical appearance of the dog with tacking in place is one to which some owners object; nevertheless, the hope is that it will give the dog time to mature and thus avoid a future, more involved surgical repair.

To prevent the sutures from being torn out, the dog should be prevented from pawing at the eye area or rubbing it against something. Littermates should not be allowed to play roughly or pull at the suture strings that may hang down from the eyelid.

The owner should be alert for signs of complications, although these are rare according to most vets. An increase in redness, an increase in swelling beyond the normal amount, increased or continued eye weeping, and squinting indicate that all is not well. A check by the vet is in order. Any drainage should be regarded with suspicion. The typical animal, after the initial post-operative swelling has subsided, is not even aware that the sutures are in place. He should be a normal, happy, active dog.

Another initial method of treating entropion is to suture the eyelids closed for one to three weeks. This method, called tarrsorhaphy, is done only on young puppies. The theory is that the technique will allow the dog to grow while protecting the eye. As can be imagined, this is an extreme approach and some data has come out that indicates these puppies may have future sight problems due to the lack of visual stimulation. More vets are electing to use tacking for their cases, but, again, each animal requires individual evaluation.

If the animal is older, six months and up, or the damage is severe, a more permanent method of treatment is appropriate since growing out of the problem is less likely. The type of correction is determined by where the entropion is positioned on the eyelid, the amount of inward roll, and the underlying cause.

Before any surgery is performed, the vet must determine exactly how much tissue needs to be removed. Obviously if the dog is in pain, he may not be able to cooperate with the vet's examination. The very act of squinting can dramatically alter the position and degree of the entropion. In order to better evaluate the dog, a topical anesthetic is placed into the eye so that the dog is relieved of any discomfort. This will, in most cases, eliminate any muscle spasm or distortion of the eye or eyelid area. From this examination, the vet is able to clearly define the areas which need treatment.

Most cases will require the removal of only the eyelid skin tissue. In severe cases, especially those with chronic spastic entropion, removal of part of the orbicularis oculi muscle could also be necessary.

Once the decision is made that surgery is necessary, the pre-operative care by the owner begins eight to twelve hours prior to surgery. Again, since general anesthesia is used for this procedure, the withholding of food and fluids helps to prevent post-operative complications of pneumonia or choking.

In most cases, a surgical technique called the modified Hotz-Celsus method is used. A small incision is made at the area of entropion, extending slightly past that point in both directions. The ends of the first incision are joined by a crescent-shaped second incision. The two incisions together form either a "smiley face" or a "frown face" pattern, depending on where the area is located. The tissue inside the crescent is removed and the two incision lines are then sutured together. This in effect takes a "tuck" out of the extra lid tissue and pulls the eyelid margin outward. By using the Hotz-Celsus technique, the vet is able to take tucks from wherever the dog requires: upper, lower or lateral lid areas. The amount of tissue removed is minimal, with most vets believing that they would rather under-correct, and possibly need two surgeries, than over-correct.

Post-operative care begins once the dog is alert and aware after the anesthesia. He should be allowed to relieve himself on leash. His bed should be in a place that allows him peace and quiet, away from family traffic and other pets. He may be groggy for a few hours, so avoiding stairs is recommended. The dog will usually be sent home wearing an Elizabethan collar to prevent the dog from scratching or rubbing the surgical site. An Elizabethan collar often presents temporary difficulties for some dogs. They may at first be frightened by the device, shaking their heads and attempting to back out of it. By calmly reassuring the dog, the owner will help him to accept the collar. In a few hours the dog will have forgotten that the collar is on him; he may then walk into doorways or objects, by catching the rim of the collar. With time, the dog will become proficient at maneuvering with the collar. At no time should the collar be removed unless under vet instructions. Dogs adjust much faster when the collar is kept on continuously. If they discover that the collar can come off, that goal becomes their first priority! Since the eye sutures can be torn out of the lid in one swipe of the paw, wearing the collar is the lesser of the two problems.

For the first two to four days after surgery, the eyes may actually look over-corrected due to the swelling pushing the lid farther out than normal. Swelling begins to recede by the third to fifth day. Antibiotic or steroid ointment placed in the eye three to four times a day will help in promoting the healing and decreasing the swelling. Cold packs may also be ordered. Placed on the site two or three times in the first 24 hours post-op, they not only reduce the swelling but aid in the comfort of the animal.

Once the swelling has resolved, the dog's appearance will begin to look more normal. It is at this point that the vet evaluates the results of the surgery. If, in a severe case, the surgery did not remove enough of the eyelid tissue, plans for future surgery are begun. The initial surgery must be totally healed and the dog fully recovered before further surgery can be performed. Hopefully, the surgery is completely successful and additional efforts are unnecessary.

At approximately ten to fourteen days after surgery, the sutures will be removed by the vet. Once the sutures are removed, the collar is also discarded. The dog is then allowed to return to more normal activities and its playmates. Some vets continue the eye ointment for another few days. A final check-up seven days later should find the dog happy and playful, no longer hampered by the discomfort of entropion.

ANTERIOR UVEITIS

Uveitis is a general term for inflammation of the iris, ciliary body or choroid eye area. The inflammation may be bilateral or unilateral, affecting one or all of these bodies. Anterior uveitis referrs specifically to an inflammation of the iris or ciliary body. It can be caused by a bacteria, virus, fungus, or chronic, untreated corneal ulcer. In the Shar-Pei, untreated entropion causing a corneal ulcer may in turn lay the foundation for anterior uveitis.

The onset of the symptoms of anterior uveitis may be sudden. The dog typically displays squinting, sensitivity to light, a cloudiness of the chamber behind the cornea, and a thickened iris. If only one eye is affected, the pupils may be of different sizes, the affected pupil being markedly constricted. The dog is in ob-

vious pain and may paw or rub the eye area. Veterinary treatment is required. As with most eye conditions, home treatment is not recommended due to the possibility of permanent vision loss.

Anterior uveitis is a medical menace, as it can set the stage for a progression of increasingly serious eye conditions. It can cause adhesions that bind the iris to the underside of the cornea or lens. Uveitis can also be the initiating cause of both cataracts and glaucoma. This potential is serious since glaucoma can cause permanent blindness in a matter of days if the condition is not treated.

Due to the severe ramifications of this disease process, treatment is typically aggressive. Systemic treatment is usually given along with a topical eye ointment. Amoxicillin or another broadspectrum antibiotic is the systemic drug of choice. Antibiotic-steroid eye ointments are frequently applied and, if necessary, a systemic anti-inflammatory drug, such as prednisolone, prednisone or aspirin, may also be required. With immediate treatment, however, the prognosis is good.

CATARACT

A cataract is a clouding of the eye's lens, which sits just behind the iris. The healthy lens is completely clear and transparent. Its role is to bend and focus

An adorable five week old with clear eyes. Betsy Davison, breeder.

the light rays that enter the eye so that they fall on the retina, at the rear of the eyeball. Cataracts do not change or affect the pupil; instead, the changes are confined to the lens' transparency. Any distortion of its clarity will ultimately cause deterioration of the quality of vision.

Cataracts may be present at birth, or caused from injury, or old age. Cataracts may also be caused by disease processes such as uveitis and diabetes. It is typically a progressive condition that worsens with time.

Obviously, there is little that can be done to prevent the eye changes of old age. The impact of cataracts due to injury or disease can be managed by conscientious owners and prompt veterinary treatment. However, the implications of congenital cataract are of concern for many breeds, including the Shar-Pei.

Congenital and juvenile early-onset cataracts are among the most significant inherited ocular conditions found in the dog. Any opacity of the lens, especially in a young animal, should be viewed as inherited unless other underlying medical conditions are present. The presence of congenital cataracts should eliminate that specific animal from any breeding program. Researchers are investigating this inherited tendency toward congenital cataracts in the Shar-Pei, although the exact method of transmission has not been determined.

The theory is that congenital cataracts begin during the early development of the fetus's eye structure. For some unknown reason, a flaw at this stage creates the groundwork for a faulty lens by changing the len's normal architecture. This imperfection in the lens may only be a small speck, which would not severely limit vision, or may encompass the entire lens, causing complete blindness. To complicate matters, this blemished area may stay at its original size or may increase in scope over time. For this reason, dogs with cataracts are monitored frequently over their lifetime. Fortunately, most congenital cataracts do not enlarge to such a degree as to completely obliterate vision.

If sight is threatened, however, and other structures in the eye are normal, surgical removal of the lens may be advisable. Dogs that have their lens removed do well in day-to-day activities. A dog's normal eyesight is not as acute as a human's. (Dogs are believed to be both near-sighted and color blind.) As a result, they naturally fine-tune their other senses. With removal of the lens, the dog will retain much of his sight although the sharp detail of objects is lost. His other keen senses will help him to compensate.

Post-surgical care is similar to any other eye surgery: care must be taken to prevent the dog from scratching or rubbing the operative site. The eye(s) may be bandaged to "rest" the eye during the healing process. An Elizabethan collar is worn for further protection. Many veterinary hospitals will keep the dog for a few days after the surgery. This is definitely advisable if no one will be able to supervise the dog at home. Close supervision of the dog is necessary for at least a few days post-op.

If the dog has been without sight for a period of time prior to surgery, care must be taken to allow the dog to adjust to his new vision. Stairs and other dangerous situations must be avoided until the dog regains his depth perception. Even judgment of distances can be in error for a time after a successful cataract surgery. In all, treatment of cataracts is highly successful, with most dogs subsequently able to lead fully active lives.

CHERRY EYE

The dog's eye, unlike man's, is protected by a third eyelid, called the nictating membrane, or the "haw." Its purpose is to protect and clean the eyeball as it sweeps across the surface. In some breeds of dogs and cats, the haw is more visible due to the shape of the eyeball or the degree of pigmentation in the membrane itself. In the healthy animal, the membranes are retracted and relatively obscure at the nasal side of the eyes.

Cherry eye is the inflammation and enlargement of a gland on the nictating membrane. As the tissue swells, it begins to protrude out of its normal, recessed position in the eye's corner. It appears as an angry, reddened mass that may become so swollen that it can cover the eyeball up to the pupil. In this exposed position, the gland is subject to further irritation, drying and inflammation.

This condition usually occurs in younger dogs, although the older dog is not immune. The Shar-Pei seem to have a higher than normal tendency toward this condition. It may be unilateral but may occur in the second eye as well. The dog exhibits minimal symptoms, a weeping discharge from the eye typically being the first sign the owner will notice. Unlike some eye disorders, cherry eye causes only mild discomfort.

Due to the chronic nature of cherry eye, and the unattractive appearance of the dog, treatment is required. If the gland is inflamed, topical antibiotic/anti-inflammatory treatment may be given for two to ten days—although topical treatment is usually unsuccessful. Surgical treatment under general anesthesia will then follow.

Two surgical techniques are currently used. The newest technique is to take the gland and tack it down on to the deeper tissues of the eye. This returns the gland to its original position and, hopefully, will eliminate any on-going irritation. An alternate method of treatment is to completely remove the gland while the membrane nictitans itself is retained. It was found that removal of the gland also removes the major source of "tears." This, in later life, could cause what is known as a "dry eye" disorder where the eye has insufficient lubrication, requiring treatment.

In the past, the entire gland and membrane were removed. Because of the side effects, this complete a procedure is now usually reserved only for malignancies of the third eyelid structures.

Ophthalmologic antibiotic/steroid ointments are used for seven to ten days following the surgery. After surgical intervention, the prognosis is good.

Thriving Shar-Pei puppies. Yao'Shu's Cloisonne X Da Hei Xiong puppies. Margery Denton, photo.

CHAPTER THREE

DERMATOLOGIC DISORDERS

HYPERSENSITIVITY

Conditions such as allergic inhalant dermatitis, flea bite allergy, and food allergies are common in the Shar-Pei. The Shar-Pei is not alone, since allergic response problems constitute the most frequent reason for any dog owner to seek veterinary assistance.

Hypersensitivity in the dog, as in humans, is the result of a physical reaction to a substance that the body views as foreign. The body is being constantly exposed to an assortment of substances that are ordinarily viewed as harmless.

For some unknown reason dogs, as well as humans, sometimes react to a harmless substance as if it were a possible enemy. This substance, or allergen, is in essence put on a "suspect list": the cells generate a memory of that substance and will be prepared for its reappearance. Should the substance reappear, the body will respond in a tangible manner, the allergic reaction. Although the allergen is not directly responsible for the response, it is the triggering factor. Viewed another way, once exposed to a questionable element, the cells create a sort of "lock and key" system:

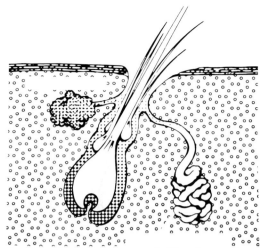

Canine skin. Courtesy of Allerderm, Inc., Colleyville, Texas.

the cell's memory of the substance is the "lock," additional allergen exposure serves as the "key" to "open" the allergic process. This lock-and-key process of identification and defense is called sensitization.

Whether the allergen gains entrance to the body by way of the respiratory, gastrointestinal or skin systems, the allergic reaction may be uncomfortable for the host. The dog may respond with a variety of physical symptoms not unlike man: sneezing, runny eyes, coughing or skin eruptions, depending on the entry site, the sensitized organ, and the individual dog's response. The more frequent the exposure to the foreign substance, or the larger the dose of allergen, the more exaggerated is the response.

Research indicates that an hereditary sensitivity to a particular allergen may be evident in certain lines within a breed. They also believe that specific individual animals within a sensitive line may exhibit an even greater sensitivity. With repeated exposure, these ultra-reactive dogs have the greatest degree of clinical difficulty. In these cases, the extreme response of the allergen-antibody reaction becomes a disease process in it-

self. Simply, the dog's reaction injures its own healthy tissues in an attempt to eliminate the foreign substance.

Steroids are the most effective anti-inflammatory treatment used to break this cycle of exaggerated allergic irritation. Oral administration is most commonly used, as topical steroids have a limited use in conditions that involve large body areas.

ALLERGIC INHALANT DERMATITIS

Allergic inhalant dermatitis, or atopy, is a common, strongly inherited disease prevalent in as much as 80% of the entire dog population. Either sex may be equally affected. Breeds that have unusually sensitive skin characteristics are especially prone to this disease, such as the West Highland White Terrier, Golden Retriever, Irish Setter, Wirehaired Fox Terrier, Scottish Terrier, Poodle, Dalmatian, Dachshund and Shar-Pei.

In the human an inhaled allergen can trigger the annoying symptoms of hay fever with sneezing, runny nose, watery eyes, and respiratory symptoms; oddly, however, the dog responds to the same inhaled allergen by exhibiting localized or generalized skin reactions. Atopy is characterized by random skin eruptions on the feet, face, ears, neck, lower abdomen, flank and underarm areas. The owner will usually notice sudden face rubbing, paw licking, chewing or generalized scratching.

The offending antigen may be a tree, grass or flower pollen, mold spore, or house dust. While most reactions involve inhaling the allergen, they can also cause symptoms if swallowed or placed in contact with the skin. The appearance of an allergen causes a release of histamine from the dog's cells, a part of the allergic "lock and key" process. (See Hypersensitivity) The histamine is the cause of the intense atopic itch. The dog scratches or bites, causing further irritation and skin damage. The skin will appear reddened, may be devoid of fur, and feel unusually warm to the touch. The dog may continually lick the spot. The surface of the inflamed skin eventually begins to break down from the constant abuse. There is usually a small amount of clear drainage without pus or odor, unless the site has a secondary bacterial infection.

Although inheritance sets the stage for a dog's sensitivity, it is generally believed that an entire season of exposure to an offending irritant is needed before a dog will exhibit this hypersensitivity. For this reason the most frequently affected dogs are in the one- to three-yearold bracket.

Atopy usually begins as a seasonal condition. In some parts of the country, the progression of possible offending allergens seems unending: March finds the tree pollens beginning, followed by the grass pollens which continue into July; in July the mold content of the air increases, with ragweed pollens beginning soon thereafter; ragweed may last well into September, while molds may remain until December. As a dog becomes increasingly sensitized to various allergens, he may begin to react to other items as well, such as house dust, wool and even materials found in home furnishing, such as kapok. In some animals, the condition can become chronic, no longer having ties with the seasonal changes.

Dr. Warren Anderson, D.V.M., in his writing for the Ralston Purina Company, suggests some practical ways the owner can minimize the impact of allergens. He suggests keeping dogs away from areas of concentrated pollen or spores, such as woodlands, fields and meadows. Obviously, daily jogging or picnics in the country with an atopic dog are not recommended. A home air purifier may help decrease the degree of reaction.

House dust, although more difficult to handle, can be minimized by keeping a room as free from dust as possible and limiting the dog to that room. In that room, remove all but the essential pieces of furniture since furniture harbors dust. Use washable cotton covers on whatever furniture is in the room. Avoid kapok stuffing if at all possible. Keep clothing or shoes that have been outdoors, away from that room. Use cotton-covered foam rubber cushions for the dog's bedding. Finally, make sure that the area is dry and warm; basements or outdoor kennels are obviously not the location of choice for atopic dogs.

The owner should begin by keeping a diary of the animal's condition. Since the causative factor may be obscure, examining a detailed history may give the first clue as to the cause. The owner should note the date when symptoms began. Are the symptoms intermittent or constant? Did the symptoms begin slowly and gradually worsen, or did they suddenly appear? Did the animal have any changes in its environment: changes in food, field trips, even new plants added to the home? Outside factors such as skin abrasion, cold, heat, or anything that causes dry skin can further aggravate the problem. Emotional stress such as kenneling or changes in lifestyle can trigger or worsen an episode. Quite often removing the causative factor from the animal's environment is not feasible.

Since repeated scratching can cause further trauma, initial treatment is directed at the control of the intense itching. Topical steroid/antibiotic ointment or cream is applied directly onto the lesions. The skin can be soaked with a soothing solution such as Domeboro's. Cool compresses held to the area can temporarily relieve the discomfort. To dry an animal with atopy, care should be taken not to rub the skin, but to softly pat it dry. Flea and tick treatments should not be used on an animal with large areas of atopy. Smaller atopic skin lesions must be carefully avoided if one is using flea or tick medication.

While humans respond well to the use of antihistamines, they are usually not effective in the treatment of the dog. The usual canine regime consists of either short term drug therapy or a long term desensitization program. Systemic steroids are particularly effective in controlling a severe condition.

Systemic steroids may be given by the oral or slow-release injection route, depending on the severity of the case. With either method, the dose amount is carefully determined. If oral treatment is followed, once the condition is under control, the amount in each dose is gradually and carefully decreased over a period of time until the symptoms are controlled with the least amount of drug. In general, the goal of steroids is to use the least amount of drug as infrequently as possible. In steroids, more is not necessarily better.

The adrenal glands in dog and man naturally produce their own steroids for use in times of stress or danger. With artificial doses of this drug, the dog's adrenal glands become ''lazy'' and rapidly decrease the amount of steroids they produce on their own. If after long-term daily use the drug is suddenly stopped, the dog may go into a form of life-threatening shock called adrenal crisis. For this reason, once the animal is no longer reacting, most vets will arrange a dosage schedule to be given every other day in order to allow the dog's own adrenals to function. Regardless, all changes in the drug or unusual stress in the animal's environment should be reported to the veterinarian immediately.

Systemic steroids such as prednisolone or prednisone are highly successful in treating the sporadic, seasonal reactions that are active for four to six months of the year. However, due to the dire side effects such as increased urination, thirst, hunger, skin changes, muscular weakness, liver damage and the threat of adrenal crisis, year-long use is not recommended.

Skin testing of suspected allergens can be done. It begins with a series of injections made just under the top layer of skin with a solution of the various suspected allergens. These injections are given on a shaven abdomen where they are carefully marked and observed for unusual reactions. The dog does not need to be sedated. Most vets have the owner calmly restrain the dog in a side-lying position. If the animal has a sensitivity to an allergen, the skin at the injection site will respond with redness and itching within 20 minutes. If there are a large number of allergens that need to be tried, the test may be divided into two sessions approximately one week apart. This testing procedure, however, is not always completely accurate. Many times a specific allergen cannot be identified. An animal may have an existing sensitivity but fails to respond at the test site. In this case, the owner's diary is invaluable.

A new method of allery testing involves the drawing of the dog's blood and testing for immunogloblins. If for example, the veterinarian is testing specifically for flea bite allergy, he would be searching for the ''flea saliva antigen'' in the dog's blood. If the dog's blood demonstrated the presence of that antigen, it would indicate the potential for an allergy to flea bite. This method, while just becoming routinely available, appears to be highly successful in pinpointing specific allergens.

For the severe or chronic condition that continues over six months of the year, the only choice of treatment is the process of hyposensitization, or desensitization. Once skin testing or blood testing has identified the offending allergen, the animal is given small injected doses of the very allergen that is causing the difficulty. Over time, the amount of allergen in each dose is increased as the individual develops a greater tolerance. This process helps the dog to develop an immunity by deactivating the allergen with an antibody before it has a chance to be "recognized" by the cell and histamine released. The goal is to have the animal at such a level that he will not respond to the allergen in his environment, or at least will respond in only a limited degree. The procedure may require many injections spread over many months.

For most owners this process may mean a daily journey to the vet's office, taxing both dog and owner. Many vets have thus begun to instruct owners on the principle and technique of giving the injections to their pet. Injection kits made by the drug manufacturers provide all the necessary solutions of allergens required. (Any combination of allergen solution can be custom-created if needed; however, a word of caution is to provide *at least* eight weeks of lead-time for special allergen solution re-orders.) The vet should write out a detailed dosage schedule that must be adhered to faithfully. Bringing the dog when the owner picks up the kit can provide an opportunity to give an injection under the vet's supervision.

Desensitization is a time-consuming, sometimes costly affair and, unfortunately, not every animal reacts as hoped. The rate of success is around 60% within the general dog population; however, there are certain breeds, or even lines within a breed, that do not respond at all to this regime. Fortunately, the Shar-Pei as a whole seems does seem to respond well to this sort of treatment as compared to the average dog population.

Most dogs are able to live a full and active life if the owner is willing to make the added effort that is required to care for an atopic dog. In reality, other than desensitization, there is no cure for atopy, only control of the symptoms.

FOOD ALLERGIES

In dogs and humans there may be some food items that cause an allergic reaction upon their consumption. In the dog even a specific brand of dog food may trigger an unwarranted reaction. This reaction is slightly different from most other allergic responses in that the symptoms, although generally spread across the body in an overall rash, may also be confined to "target organs," such as feet pads or ear canals. Even more confusing, the only sign that something is amiss may be that the dog vomits a few hours after feeding. In some cases, there may be mucus or blood-tinged diarrhea. Although this sort of allergic problem is infrequent in the dog, some Shar-Pei do appear to be sensitive to specific foods.

Strangely, many dogs seem to have an intolerance of beef, milk and soybean products. Many breeders indicate that soy in particular seems to be a problem for the Shar-Pei. Since beef and soy are the bases for many commercial dog foods, both canned and dry, the owner must then locate a quality food that does not contain these items. A few dry dogs foods have recently been developed that use chicken and/or lamb as the protein supply and rice as the carbohydrate source; they have been helpful in treating dogs with beef and/or soy sensitivity.

Of all of the allergies, this kind of allergy is one of the most difficult to diagnose due to the unspecific reaction pattern that dogs exhibit. The dog, having repeated, frequent exposure to the allergen, is chronically symptomatic. Unfortunately, the symptoms do not respond well to steroids, and the large body area makes topical medications difficult to apply.

Removal of the offending food item is the first step in treating the dog. The approach must be totally structured and unbending; a *single* dietary indiscretion can eliminate weeks of detective work!

items are gradually added to test the dog's tolerance until a healthy diet is created. Any offending food substance must be completely avoided. This program should be structured by the vet who will be in close contact with the owner for updates on the dog's reactions. In most cases, the dog must remain on this special collection of food items, or the D/D diet, for the remainder of its life. Even small or accidental indiscretions will cause a relapse.

The following recipe and instructions are courtesy of Hill's Company.

Canine Hypoallergenic Diet:
¼ lb. diced lamb
1 cup cooked rice
1 teaspoon corn oil
1 ½ teaspoons dicalcium phosphate
Balanced vitamin-mineral supplement in a quantity sufficient to provide the daily requirement for each vitamin and trace mineral.

Trim fat from lamb. Cook thoroughly (braise or roast) without seasoning. Add remaining ingredients and mix well. Keep covered in refrigerator. Yield: ¾ lb.

Analysis:

Protein	10.0%
Fat	8.0%
Carbohydrate	15.3%
Moisture	65.0%
Calories	800 Kcal/lb

Feeding Guide:
Feed sufficient amount to maintain normal body weight.

Body Weight	Approx. Daily Feeding
5 lb.	⅓ lb.
10 lb.	½ lb.
20 lb.	1 lb.
40 lb.	1 ½ lb.
60 lb.	2 lb.
80 lb.	2 ½ lb.
100 lb.	3 lb.

First the dog is placed on an hypoallergenic canine diet that can be purchased (the Hill's D/D Diet) or may be prepared at home from scratch. This is composed of lamb and rice; a typical dog would not have been exposed to these items since they are not commonly included in dog food. No spices, garlic, salt, table scraps, treats or vitamin supplements are allowed. The dog remains on this diet for three weeks while his system "clears" itself of its irritation. If the problem is one of food intolerance, the dog should begin to improve while on this menu. Once the dog is free of symptoms, one food item is added to his diet at a time. The dog's new diet will include the added food for at least five days. Typically the first item to be added is chicken, followed by wheat, etc. If the dog should begin to show signs of reaction after adding a particular food substance, it is a good bet that this may be the, or one of the, offending item(s). The dog should then return to the hypoallergenic diet until all signs of the reaction disappear. Once again, food

If the allergy is suspected to be food induced, maintain the patient on this diet and distilled water. Then expose the patient to foods, one at a time, beginning with tap water, to discover the offending materials. The aim is determine food the patient CAN eat rather than those the patient cannot eat.

FLEA BITE ALLERGY

The most aggravating and sometimes frustrating battle on the hands of the conscientious owner is the control of the flea. The flea seems to scoff at our most diligent efforts to rid him from our house and pet. All sorts of solutions and preventative methods have been devised—with the score still in favor of the little flea! In the semi-tropical areas of our country, control becomes a year-long battle. For the sensitive dog who reacts to the flea's bite with an allergic reaction, it becomes a very serious matter.

Fleas are wide spread throughout the animal world, domesticated or wild. Deer, raccoon, mice, wolves, fox, rabbits, squirrels and bobcats all suffer from these pests. It is unknown how many wild animals suffer from flea bite allergy, but in the domesticated dog it is a major cause of skin disease.

The primary symptom is intense itching in the dorsal aspect of the lumbar or the inguinal areas. The skin first begins to look reddened. This is followed by the appearance of small raised pimples. A thick crust or scab may form over the lesion. Hair is lost from around the inflamed area. The dog is in acute distress, licking and biting at the spot, perhaps even rolling on the floor in an attempt to gain relief. Over time, if the condition persists, the skin will turn thick and darken in color.

Studies have now proven that the adult stage of the flea's life cycle is actually a very small period of time. Most of the flea's life, as egg and larva, are spent in the environment. The adult flea hops onto the animal only for feeding. The flea bites the dog in order to feed on the blood of its dog-host. It is not the presence of the flea on the skin that causes the reaction, but the injection of the flea's saliva into the dog's skin as the flea bites. Contrary to popular belief, the flea does not bite in self-defense as the dog scratches, tickled by the movement of the flea through the dog's coat. In the sensitive dog, even one fleabite may start an allergic response.

1. Adult flea — can live for 2 years without feeding

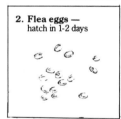

2. Flea eggs — hatch in 1-2 days

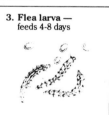

3. Flea larva — feeds 4-8 days

4. Larva spins cocoon — adult emerges in 5 days or less

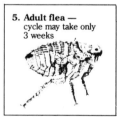

5. Adult flea — cycle may take only 3 weeks

Life Cycle of the Flea. Courtesy of Vet-Kem, Dallas, Texas.

The first step in the treatment of the dog is removal of the flea. This is not a simple task. One trip to the pet supply store will find the owner overwhelmed by the array of dips, solutions, sprays, powders, collars, tags, supplements, traps, foggers and noise devices to combat this tiny creature. To complicate issues, some compounds can not be used together with other compounds, or the dog will be made ill. Some medical conditions, such as atopy, require extremely careful use of any flea treatment of any variety and only under the direction of a veterinarian. Whenever treating a dog for fleas, it should be remembered that all of these products are potent chemicals and must be treated with caution and respect. Many owners have inadvertently harmed the dog in their overzealous attempt to help.

The first action is to attempt to make the dog more comfortable by preventing the flea from biting the dog. Dipping and shampooing the dog is a reasonable method that can be used during the routine bath. Flea shampoos should be used with care, preventing any from entering into the dog's eyes. Sterile eye ointments placed in the eyes before bathing can prevent inadvertent eye irritation. Similarly, cotton balls placed in the ears before bathing can prevent the chemicals from triggering an ear inflammation. If the shampoo or dip must be diluted, follow the directions carefully. Dips are applied after the shampoo has been rinsed. They are allowed to dry on the coat and create a long-lasting barrier. Dips are highly concentrated solutions that last for five to seven days in the average dog. Some dogs are sensitive to certain dips and may develop a secondary skin rash. In this event, the vet can suggest a product that is less irritating. Some manufacturing companies make shampoos and dips that are compatible and are meant to be used together. If there is any question as to whether a shampoo and dip are compatible, contact your vet for advice.

For the short coated Shar-Pei, a good quality flea powder or spray is inexpensive, easy to apply and has good residual effect. A good quality flea powder kills the flea before he has time to feed. Care must be taken with sprays as they are highly concentrated and can cause a toxic drug level, especially in an older animal, if ingested.

Flea collars and tags, while popular with the public, have not been shown to be very effective. In addition, some Shar-Pei have a sensitivity to the chemicals that are in the collar. These dogs will have hair loss and reddened, irritated skin around the collar area. Under no circumstances should flea collars and dips be used together!

In the latest research, the new ultrasonic flea collars have just recently been proven to be effective. Although studies are still underway, the collar appears to function best when used in conjunction with adequate environmental flea control.

Some dog owners concerned with the amount of chemicals used in conventional flea treatment endorse the natural route. There is an assortment of herbal collars, dips, shampoos, oral supplements and sprays available. To date they have a controversial effectiveness rate.

Along the same non-chemical line there are flea traps that lure the little pests onto sticky paper by beckoning night lights, and ultrasonic room defenders that reportedly drive the fleas away by noxious sound levels. Garlic and Brewer's Yeast rank as the only food items devoted to flea control. The theory behind the use of yeast is that it changes the taste of the dog's blood or skin, therefore discouraging the flea from biting.

At the other end of the spectrum, an anti-flea drug, called Spot-On, is available for flea control. It is applied between the shoulderblades and absorbed into the bloodstream. It is an organic phosphate and has some practitioners concerned with the possible long-term side effects. Proban, an oral form of systemic flea control, has been on the market for a number of years. At this point, use of Proban is used mostly in the semi-tropical climates where year-round control is required.

Whenever using a ''blood-barrier'' flea

product, it should be remembered that the flea must bite the animal at least once in order to be repelled. In the highly allergic animal, one bite may cause an allergic response. For this reason, items such as garlic, yeast, Spot-on and Pro-ban may not be of use in these sensitive dogs.

The most effective control method, and the least frequently done, is treating the dog's environment. Since the flea life cycle is primarily in the environment more often than on the dog, treatment of the yard, house and its furnishings is imperative. Inside treatment can take the form of fogging sprays that penetrate all the little hiding places: footboards, carpeting, and upholstery. Care must be taken to protect food and cooking items from contamination with the fog; otherwise the food must be discarded and the cooking utensils thoroughly washed. All people and pets must be removed from the premises during the fogging. The manufacturer's directions on how long to remain out of the home should be taken seriously! Fogging will be needed two to four times per year depending on the climate. Washing of the dog's bedding and frequent vacuuming, with immediate disposal of the vacuum bag, will also be of help. An alternate approach is to place some flea powder into the vacuum bag prior to cleaning the pet's area.

Another new product on the market are microencapsulated chemical sprays which replace the older fogging methods. These sprays are time-released thereby having a greater length of effectiveness. There are forms that can be applied directly onto the yard, house or pet and will remain effective regardless of environmental conditions such as rainwater or vacuuming. If research indicates that these products are as effective as hoped, they could mean an important breakthrough in this battle.

For the allergic dog, topical steroid creams will help to relieve the itching.

Any secondary bacterial skin infections can be treated with a combination steroid/antibiotic preparations. For the severely affected dog, systemic steroids may be needed during flea season. As with any use of a systemic steroid, careful monitoring of the dog will be required. For the dog that does not respond well to systemic treatment or who lives with a year-long problem, a program of desensitization injections might be beneficial. (See Atopy)

DEMODICOSIS

Demodex canis is a large name for a little mite that normally resides in the hair follicles, oil and sweat glands of the dog, wild animals and, occasionally, man. Although it is estimated that all dogs harbor the parasite, the demodex disease is a matter of severity and the individual dog's response. Should the population of mites become uncontrolled, then a condition called demodicosis, or demodetic mange, occurs. This infestation may involve only localized areas or the entire body. While localized demodex is a nuisance, the generalized form is life-threatening. Many breeds are susceptible to this disease; the Shar-Pei appears to be particularly prone.

The demodex mite is a parasite that goes through various stages of development in its progression toward adulthood. It begins as a spindle-shaped egg which soon hatches into a larva with three short pairs of legs. This larval stage then moves through two further stages where the developing parasite adds on another pair of legs. As it continues to mature, a head, chest, four pairs of legs and a long, striated abdomen finally emerge. Even at the adult stage the mite can be seen only under a microscope. The entire life cycle of a mite is from 20 to 35 days and occurs completely within the confines of the host's skin pores. Adult mites cannot survive off the host.

The cells and debris of the hair follicles are the main source of nutrients for the mite. As it feeds, it begins to undermine the integrity of the follicle and surrounding skin. Hair loss occurs in a patchy, rounded fashion, similar to ringworm. The surrounding skin becomes swollen and red, with crusts forming on the oozing sites. In localized cases, the most common sites are the muzzle, face and foreleg areas. In the generalized form, the entire body may be covered with bleeding or draining lesions. Clinical symptoms of the disease are usually apparent within several months of exposure. These lesions are susceptible to secondary infection by bacteria such as *staphylococci, pseudomonas or proteus.*

Transmission occurs directly from one host to another. The mite is only on top of the skin when moving from one hair follicle to another. During this time, while on the skin's surface, it may have access to other sites or to other animals. Particularly as the dog licks or chews his skin, a mite can transfer to new locations. Transmission of the mite frequently occurs during playtime between animals. Although newly born animals are free of the mite immediately upon birth, dams transmit the mite to their newborn pups as they nurse and climb on her. Mites have been found on newborns within 16 hours of birth. Littermates infect each other as they nestle for sleep or rough-house together. Fortunately for the owner, the demodex canis does not transfer readily to man!

Localized demodex is a mild condition comprising one to five small, distinct, hairless patches of skin most commonly found around the eyes and folds of the mouth. Occasionally, areas will be found on the trunk or rear legs of the dog. They may or may not be itchy and they have normal pigmentation. Secondary infections of the patches are uncommon. Fortunately, only 10% of the localized cases develop into the more ominous generalized form.

Generalized demodex may begin as a localized infestation that eventually becomes an all-encompassing condition involving not only a local skin response but a total body reaction to the mite invasion. It is one of the most severe of skin diseases. With generalized demodex, the current theory is that the dog has an inherent T-cell defect that hinders the animal's normally protective response to any parasite. T-cells are responsible for the immunity of the animal at the cell level. In demodex the number of T-cells available is normal, but for some reason they do not function properly. As the mites proliferate beyond the animal's ability to control them, the body's defense mechanism begins to deteriorate even further under the constant assault. The follicles become veritable incubators for the mite's rapid reproduction rate. Secondary bacterial infections may further depress the animal's resistance. These animals are in pain and acutely ill. To complicate the condition, it is believed that, as the mites increase, their presence and/or the secondary skin infections somehow create a suppressive factor in the host's blood that further inactivates the animal's immune system. The disease process becomes a vicious cycle: defective T-cells allow an increase in mites and infection, which creates a deviant blood factor, which further defeats the T-cells, thus allowing more mites to survive. It has been proven that when a rampant mite population has been eradicated, the animal's immune system returns to normal. Unfortunately, while the exact mechanism behind this immunological-blocking action is not understood, it is known that the tendency for generalized demodex is an inherited trait.

Within generalized demodex there are three varieties: juvenile, adult onset, and chronic demodectic pododermatitis. The juvenile form occurs within the age range of three to twelve months. It rapidly

Generalized demodex.

progresses to this stage from a localized infestation. The skin easily bleeds, loses its elasticity, and has a foul odor. The lesions are found around the head and neck, and are extremely painful. Lymph glands in the face, forearms and feet are acutely swollen. The animals are typically lethargic, have poor appetites, run fevers, and incessantly itch. As they scratch, the surface bacteria of the skin contaminates the wound leading to infection. Naturally, scratching further traumatizes the skin.

The adult-onset variety is usually discovered in an animal that has been otherwise healthy. Victims are usually five years of age but can be much older. The animal is extremely ill. There may be a concurrent, undiagnosed, underlying medical condition such as liver disease or hyperadrenocorticism which suppresses the dog's immune status. Studies show, however, that in the majority of adult-onset cases the animal is discovered to have a malignant neoplasm within one year of demodex diagnosis.

Apparently the malignancy depletes the dog's immune system and thus allows for the over-proliferation of the mite. Treatment of these animals is usually unsuccessful.

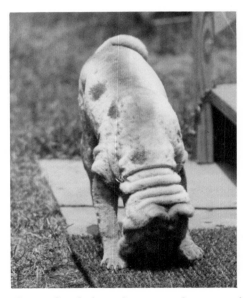

Generalized demodex on a four month old puppy.

In demodectic pododermatitis, only the feet are affected. Many cases begin as the adult generalized form but the paw sites never completely heal; infrequently this type of demodex can begin suddenly in the feet with no other sites of involvement. Due to constant exposure of the paws and interdigital skin folds to weather, soil and licking, these sites are usually complicated by severe secondary bacterial infections. Otitis externa (ear infection) is prevalent as the dog transfers both mite and bacteria to the ear as he scratches.

Other factors that may influence a generalized infestation are age, nutrition, stress or other existing disease processes. Data indicates that age and breeding appear to affect the condition in that 87% of the animals are purebred and over seven months of age. Half of the animals having generalized demodex are female and usually unspayed. Stress has been indicated as a significant triggering factor. In addition, the use of steroids in the treatment of other diseases has been implicated as a instigating factor, since steroids themselves have an immune suppressing action. As is

Feet are swollen and blackened. The condition is spreading up the legs.

true in many physical conditions, demodex appears to be an underlying, inherited tendency that becomes activated by one or more environmental elements.

Unfortunately, diagnosis of the condition may not be a straightforward procedure since the mite is a normal component of the skin. Skin scrapings or biopsy of multiple sites may be required to determine if the *numbers* of mites, rather than just their presence, is excessive. The average, normal number found in the healthy dog is one to two mites in six to ten skin scrapings. A minimum of three to five different skin sites should be chosen to determine the relative number of mites. Of most importance is that the skin immediately adjacent to the lesions be sampled since that is the "front line" of mite activity: as the mites feed, they work their way in an outward direction. The interior of the lesion, although showing physical signs of infestation, is actually only the aftermath of their destruction.

Scraping of the skin involves first removing any exudate. Crusts should be gently soaked and removed to provide access to the lesion's margin. The scapel blade is coated with a thin layer of mineral oil to trap the mites as the skin is scraped. The hair follicle should be squeezed between the thumb and forefinger to force out the mites and their debris. The collection is then placed into a drop of mineral oil on a microscope slide and observed under low power. Movement of the mouth and legs of the mite should be readily apparent. If mites are not found in a skin scraping, deeper biopsy of the hair follicle will usually confirm their presence if other clinical signs support the diagnosis. Cultures of the exudate should be performed to determine the most effective antibiotic for treatment of any secondary bacterial infections.

A hemotological evaluation should also be included in the assessment of the dog since over 50% of animals with

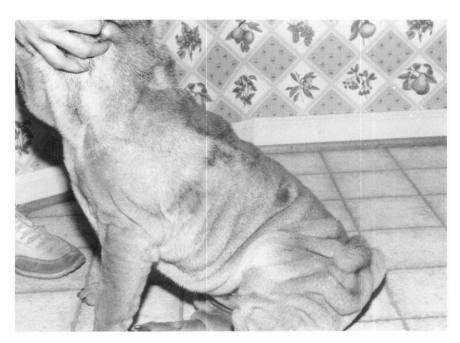

Skin lesions of generalized demodex.

generalized demodex are anemic. It is felt that this is a normal reaction to a chronic infection and is not an element of the disease itself. Treatment for severe anemia would constitute a blood transfusion.

Treatment of the localized form is currently the focus of much debate. Some practitioners feel that treatment of the localized form is unnecessary since the condition will usually self-cure within two months regardless of the medical intervention. Furthermore, other practitioners say that localized demodex should not be treated in potential breeding animals in order to determine whether or not the condition will progress to th more severe generalized form. This may be an important determination since any animal with generalized demodex should be removed from breeding consideration. Unless the disease is allowed to progress unrestricted, this consideration will be difficult to assess. For the owner, however, the withholding of treatment may be an emotionally difficult ordeal.

Clipping of the dog's coat around the sites, especially in the brush or bear-coated Shar-Pei, and removal of the crusts by hydrotherapy and bathing with benzoyl peroxide will facilitate the healing process. Mitaban (amitraz) applied to the sites is the treatment of choice for localized demodex, although Ronnel is also used in its treatment. A protective eye ointment should be instilled prior to use of either solution.

Although treatment with Ronnel has been largely replaced by Mitaban, it is still occasionally used. A Ronnel solution should be applied to less than 1/3 of the animal's body on a rotating, daily basis. Treatment of larger portions of the body area may result in toxicity and should be supervised closely due to the dangers to both animal and owner! It should not be applied to dogs that are extremely ill or elderly. The antidote for Ronnel is atropine and pralidoxime chloride (Protopam) given by injection. At present, Ronnel is not officially approved for use in dogs.

In chronic cases, the dog's skin may begin to show signs of dryness or irritation. A rinsing solution of Alpha-Keri oil can be applied. One teaspoon mixed in with a quart of warm water/Mitaban solution makes a soothing rinse.

Goodwinol, a topical medication, is also a very effective treatment for smaller sites. The owner should take care to apply the ointment in the direction of the hair growth so that a minimum of hair loss will result.

Generalized demodex is a medically challenging disease process. It responds slowly to any intervention. Fortunately, 30-50% of the juvenile form with dogs under one year of age with generalized mites will recover spontaneously. Adult onset generalized demodex, especially due to the underlying medical complications, have a much lower recovery rate.

Most practitioners recommend beginning the treatment of any generalized demodex condition with a benzoyl peroxide shampoo, such as Oxydex, to flush the mites out of the hair follicles. The foaming action of the shampoo brings the mites into direct contact with the miticidal preparations that follow.

As in the localized form, Ronnel and Mitaban may be employed. The manufacturer of Mitaban (Upjohn) provides a clear and detailed information booklet as to the application and precautions to be taken. Mitaban should be applied by completely soaking the animal once every two weeks, until two negative skin scrapings result. The average time span is a total of four to eight treatments. The owner should use rubber gloves while applying the solution. The room should be adequately ventilated. The coat should be blown dry after a treatment to maintain as much of the chemical on the hair as possible. Any exposure to water, such as swimming or rainfall, must be avoided, as it dilutes the drug's effectiveness. With any of these topical solutions, a temporary sedative effect may occur for the first 24 hours after treatment, particularly after the initial dose. Other side effects of the dip may include anorexia, vomiting, diarrhea or reddening and swelling of the skin. Any unusual or severe reactions should be reported to the vet immediately. In most cases, these side effects are temporary. As the treatment is 90% effective, Mitaban has been heralded by some owners as a "miracle" drug.

Demodectic pododermatitis is extremely resistant to treatment. While the feet are readily accessible to soaking in a miticidal solution, for some unknown reason, this form of demodex does not respond. The condition usually becomes chronic. For larger, more active animals the swelling and lesions of the feet and pads are painfully demobilizing.

The owner needs to realize that even after miticidal treatment has begun, the impact of the mites will still be seen. Hair loss and enlargment of the lesions will continue as the cellular damage has already been done; the edges of the lesions have already been undermined by the mite's activity. Once the damaged cells have been removed, the condition will begin to improve in appearance. Throughout the treatment period, repeated skin scrapings provide an accurate picture of the condition's progress.

In the past few years prognosis for animals with the juvenile form of generalized demodex has become much more optimistic. The relapse rate is quite low at 10%. Some animals require life-long Mitaban treatments in order to keep the mites to within an acceptable level for that particular dog's immune system. However, many animals return to a completely healthy condition with only superficial skin scarring as a reminder of the disease.

Researchers have just announced an additional approach to treating demodex. It has been discovered that 200mg. of Vitamin E, given orally, five times a day for six weeks can be useful in controlling demodex. As more practitioners begin to prescribe this regime, the true value of this vitamin supplementation will be seen.

The appropriate treatment of any secondary infection in generalized demodex is imperative since such infections are the primary cause of death. In all cases, systemic antibiotics are required. The antibiotics of choice are cephalosporin, chloramphenicol, erythromycin, lincomycin, or oxacillin. Smaller localized infections may be treated with Betadine soaks.

In addition, great care should be taken to shelter the dog from additional stress during his illness. Kenneling, changes in his environment, or dietary alterations should be avoided. If possible, elective surgeries should be postponed for as long as ten months. As in any severe medical illness, the animal's housing should be clean, dry, warm and away from undue noise or activity.

Should there be a recurrence of the disease, or if it occurs in a pregnant or estrous female, a hormonal influence should be suspected. The increase in estrogen during the female's estrus and/or pregnancy lowers her already decreased immune defense. In this case, hysterectomy should provide a permanent cure. Obviously, treatment with any steroids are contraindicated, as these animals are already immune suppressed.

The generalized form of this disease has important ramifications for the Shar-Pei breeder. Since the disease is an inherited tendency, breeding of an affected animal is strongly discouraged. The American Academy of Veterinary Dermatology advises neutering of all animals, male and female, who have or had generalized demodex. In this manner the prevalence of the disease can be controlled, and, hopefully, eradicated in the future.

SEBORRHEA

Due to its complexity, seborrhea is one of the most frustrating of all skin disorders for the veterinarian. In reality, it is not a disease process per se, but a classification of the skin's response. Thus seborrhea can be grouped as either a primary or secondary response. Differentiation of the two types and cause is problematic.

Primary seborrhea occurs as an idiopathic condition apart and independent from any other medical disorder. It is common to the Cocker Spaniel, Springer Spaniel, West Highland White Terrier, Basset Hound, German Shepherd, Poodle, Dachshund and Labrador Retriever. Within certain lines of these breeds there is a strong hereditary predilection. The symptoms may appear in the very young pup and last throughout its lifetime. The condition becomes increasingly severe over time and is resistant to treatment.

Secondary seborrhea is actually a condition generated by other physical factors. It is by far the most common category of seborrhea. While secondary seborrhea must be approached as a separate entity, a search for the underlying disease is also required. Some of the factors that can cause secondary seborrheic skin reactions are endocrine imbalances, nutritional deficiencies, parasite infestation, allergic sensitivity reactions, autoimmune diseases, various infectious diseases and malignancies.

As a whole, seborrhea is a fundamental disorder of the epidermal layer of the dog's skin. In normal skin, the cell layers are constantly being replaced as the top layer ages and becomes worn and is shed. This process of replacement works from the bottom skin layer toward the top in an orderly and steady fashion. The average dog replaces his epidermal layer approximately every 21 days. Any impact on the production or exchange of cells will greatly influence the type and quality of the skin. In the seborrheic dog the rate of epidermal cell turnover is every three to four days. At this exaggerated pace, the cells do not generate in an normal manner; there will be areas of clumping, thickening, irritation and scaling. To the eye, the skin is clearly not healthy.

There are three basic varieties of seborrhea based on its physical characteristics:seborrhea sicca, seborrhea oleosa and seborrheic dermatitis. An individual animal may simultaneously exhibit more than one variation. All forms may be confined to one spot, one region, or the entire animal.

Seborrhea sicca displays a dry skin pattern with either localized or diffused gray to white scaling. It may also have an unpleasant odor. The coat is dry and dull in appearance. Hair loss is profuse. Dr. Edward Baker, D.V.M., Scientific Fellow of the American Academy of Allergy and Immunology, aptly describes these animals as looking "as though they are walking or standing in a dust storm. When they leave the table, or the examination room, the area is literally covered with scale." Irish Setters, German Shepherds, Dachshunds, and Doberman Pinschers are frequently affected.

Seborrhea oleosa, the more severe form, is found predominantly in the Cocker Spaniel, Springer Spaniel, and Chinese Shar-Pei. It presents as greasy, clumped scales that cling to the dog's coat, especially on the ears, elbows and hocks. The coat itself feels oily if a hand is run in the direction of the hair growth. The odor is strong and, at times, rancid. There can be marked skin irritation which continually weeps. In many cases, a corresponding ear infection, ceremenous otitis, is also present. Localized sites are round, hairless patches which have a reddened, flaking rim, covered by a thick crust. They are found most frequently on the trunk and chest. Severe cases can involve thickening of the foot pads with inflammation of the webbing between the toes.

The Shar-Pei seems particularly troubled by this form of seborrhea due to the excessive skin folds. These folds serve to trap skin oil, sweat and exudate; lack of air flow and the irritation of the short hairs rubbing against the already beleaguered skin increase the problem. Secondary bacterial infections are common due to this ideal environment. Control of odor in these animals is difficult.

Seborrheic dermatitis is a variety found most often on the axilla, thorax and lower abdomen. It may be associated with concurrent infections of the hair follicles. The lesions are described as "bulls-eyes," having a distinct outline and a marked interior center. Inflammation is intense. Cocker Spaniels and Springer Spaniels are the most prone.

Seborrhea may be triggered by a broad range of causative factors. One of the most frequent is hypothyroidism. The thyroid hormone influences both the turnover rate of the epidermal cells as well as the amount of oil generated in the hair follicles. Although the animal may not be exhibiting other clinical signs associated with hypothyroidism, most practitioners agree that laboratory analysis should be pursued.

Hormonal imbalances are triggers for what can be either a constant or cyclical occurrence of seborrhea. The female with heat cycle disturbances, the overly aggressive intact male or animals with sex-hormone organ tumors should be suspect. One difficulty with this initiating element is that relatively few laboratory tests exist to determine the level of sex hormones in the dog. Thus, treatment may need to commence without the concrete verification of lab results.

Adrenal gland disorders may also instigate ·a seborrheic condition. This condition is found in animals with hyperadrenocorticism or in animals receiving large doses of artificial steroids.

Dietary factors have a profound impact on the skin and coat of the dog. Seemingly minor elements can create a host of epidermal disorders, including seborrhea.

• Fat intake deficiencies may cause seborrhea. At risk are dogs receiving generic brand dog food, semi-moist dog food, homemade diets and old commercial dog food that has outlived its usefulness. (For this reason, dry dog food should not be stored for longer than six months as it loses its nutritiontal value.)

• The dog requires three essential fatty acids: linoleic, arachidonic and linolenic. Deficiency in any or all of these substances can cause an initial dry, dull coat with a ''dandruff-like'' flake. If the condition persists, the oil content of the skin increases to the point that the hair becomes greasy. This deficiency may be due to omission or to faulty digestive processes, such as in malabsorption syndrome. Laboratory tests should be directed to intestinal, pancreatic or liver dysfunction.

• The dog's skin requires as much as 30% of all ingested protein. Protein deficiencies may cause a dry and brittle coat with partial hair loss on the extremities. Correction of the diet should eliminate the problem.

• If measured, Vitamin A levels may be normal but, for some reason, may be deficit for that particular animal. Thus, a relative Vitamin A deficiency presents with increased thickening of the skin of the face and pressure areas, such as the hocks, elbows and hips. Most of these animals require supplementation. Oddly, extremely levels of Vitamin A can present with symptoms similar to its lack: itching, scal-

ing, painful, swollen joints, vomiting and anorexia. A carefully analyzed history taken from the owner should make the distinction clear.

• Zinc plays an important role in protein utilization. Although uncommon, its deficiency presents with hair loss, crusting, and raw, irritated skin around the mouth, chin, eyes and ears. Animals given too much calcium may develop a secondary zinc deficiency as calcium interferes with zinc uptake. Thus, supplementation of any vitamin or mineral should always be first approved by the veterinarian.

Parasites, both internal and external, may create skin lesions. Two most common external causes of seborrhea are the flea and the demodetic mite. In either case, the eradication of the vermin should cause a resolution of skin involvement.

Food allergies or sensitivities to environmental products (Atopy) can create secondary seborrhea. Removal of the causative element, or desensitization to it, will help to terminate the condition. One unique characteristic of this sort of seborrhea is that itching almost always precedes the skin eruption.

Malignancies of the skin quite often produce a seborrheic state. This is a most difficult situation since the animal's health is already under siege. Successful treatment of the skin condition rides on the eradication of the neoplasm.

Diagnosis of such a widely varied conglomeration of causative factors is extremely difficult. The veterinarian and owner must be willing to invest time, money and effort to gradually weed through the various options until, by process of elimination, the source is pinpointed. The owner must supply accurate historical information as to the dog's diet, activity, symptoms and disease course. Something as simple as over-bathing or sensitivity to a particular soap product may be the instigator. Even an arid environment has been implicated in some dogs! In severe cases, a dermatological specialist may need to be consulted.

Diagnosis of primary, idiopathic seborrhea is in reality made after the deliberate elimination of all other causative possibilities. The goal of treating primary seborrhea is one of control rather than cure. An attempt is made to decrease the oiliness, the itching, the odor and the inflammation. This will be a lifelong process on the part of the owner.

Determination of secondary seborrhea most usually begins with laboratory testing of skin scrapings, fecal analysis, thyroid function tests, bacterial and fungal cultures, biopsy, blood chemistry, and urinalysis. Treatment of secondary seborrhea is actually a two-level process: treating the overt skin symptoms and treating the underlying medical disease. If allergies are suspected, then the food or environmental irritant must be removed (See Atopy; Flea Bite Dermatitis; Food Allergies)

Treatment of both primary and secondary seborrhea revolves around the bathtub. Warm water hydrotherapy helps in the reduction of itching and removal of exudate and scales. A hand-held shower massager is a valuable and time saving item for the owner. Domeboro's solution may be applied to local lesion sites to decrease the irritation.

Once the scales and crusts are removed, medications are then able to penetrate the skin. Medicated shampoos are especially created for this use. The best contain .5-2% sulfur, 1-3% salicylic acid, 2% tar and 2.5-3% benzoyl peroxide. With most medicated shampoos, the lather is left in contact with the coat for a minimum of 10-15 minutes and then COMPLETELY rinsed out. Vet-Derm has a shampoo that is useful in the control of seborrheic lesions as does

the Westwood Company, called Sebutone. If undue skin dryness occurs, a soothing cream or oil rinse can be applied. Alpha Keri oil or Aveeno oilated bath product are popular. In general, the owner is instructed to shampoo the dog whenever the scales or odor returns. In the initial stages, this may mean washing as frequently as every three to four days. As the condition improves, these baths may be needed only every three to four weeks. Many grooming salons will provide this bathing service. (It is recommended that the owner provide the groomer with the correct shampoo prescribed by the veterinarian.)

Ointments such as Pragmatar contain these same sulfur, tar and salicylic acid combinations. They are particularly helpful in treating any localized lesions.

Treatment of hormonally influenced seborrhea is directly related to the treatment of the glandular problem. Testicular tumors and atrophy, or ovarian imbalance, respond only to castration or ovariohysterectomy. In some cases, replacement therapy to restore normal hormonal levels has been successful.

Dietary-deficiency-induced seborrhea is the most amenable to treatment. If the defect is in the amount of fatty acids, they may be readily added to the diet: a combination of equal parts of both animal fat, such as lard or bacon grease, and vegetable fats, such as peanut, corn or safflower oil, deliver the necessary ingredients. Depending on its size, the dog is started with one to three teaspoons added to the total daily food intake. The amount of oil is slowly increased over the next few days until a soft stool occurs; then the oil dosage is slowly decreased until the stool is normal. The dosage is maintained at that amount for a minimum of eight days. If the condition is fat-related, the lesions should begin to improve.

One obvious drawback to this approach is in the obese or pancreatitis-prone animal. The obese animal should not have the additional calories and a sensitive pancreas can not tolerate a high fat diet. For these animals, restricting the oil to a maximum of one teaspoon for every cup of dry food, or can of moist, may be better tolerated. For highly sensitive animals, a powdered low-calorie form is available and should be the method of choice. In many cases, this specially formulated powder supplies a more balanced amount of fatty acids and zinc and, in some dogs, may be more effective than the homemade variety.

Treatment of any secondary bacterial or fungal infections must be addressed immediately. Oral antibiotics or fungicides are most often employed. Once infections have been cleared, then careful, monitored treatment of itching and inflammation can begin with steroids. Prednisone is used for a short-term intervention. If the dog requires longer treatment, then most practitioners will turn to an alternate-day schedule with steroids. Topical steroid ointments are confined to treating localized lesions. Once inflammation has been controlled, steroids are no longer required.

Good grooming of the seborrheic animal cannot be too strongly stressed. Daily brushing is imperative for the health of the dog. Although the combing and brushing tends to bring flakes and scales to the surface of the coat, which may be objectionable to some owners, these must be removed in order to facilitate regeneration of healthy cells. In the bear-coated Shar-Pei, clipping down of the hair in length will simplify treatment.

The prognosis for seborrhea depends greatly on the cause and its susceptibility to treatment. For some, a minor change in diet will cure the condition, whereas for some primary cases, control is the best that be hoped for.

SKIN FOLD DERMATITIS

Skin fold dermatitis, or the more severe skin fold pyoderma, is a condition generated by the characteristics of the dog's own coat. In the Shar-Pei, the abundance of wrinkles and excess tissue creates folds that are small incubators for skin bacteria. The folds retain the dog's body heat, while increased humidity from the secretions of the eyes, muzzle or vulva (in the female) adds to this ideal environment. The darkness and lack of air flow within the folds further magnify the bacterial overgrowth. As the skin's integrity begins to deteriorate, the rubbing and friction from the coat hairs themselves add to the skin's trauma.

Pyodermic skin will appear irritated and inflamed with a foul odor. If the condition is severe or neglected, pus may exude from the skin's surface as secondary infections spread deeper into the tissues. Severe inflammations may cause an elevated temperature and enlargement of the nearby lymph glands.

Essentially, anywhere the conditions are right, skin fold dermatitis can occur. In the Shar-Pei, these areas are the ventral jaw or under the lower lip where moisture from drinking or drooling keeps the area moist, the vulva where urine soiling and scald weakens the skin, and between the toes where licking and weather increase the moisture level. Interdigital dermatitis may also be seen in the dog that is kenneled outdoors on damp ground or in very humid conditions. The body folds on the trunk and flank are usually not involved due to the lower humidity and increased air flow in these areas, although heavily wrinkled Shar-Pei puppies may be affected.

Dermatitis is most difficult to cure in the jaw or lip areas due to the constant exposure to moisture. In the Shar-Pei it is possible that the younger dog will correct his own condition as he matures into the excess skin. This may be a difficult wait for the puppy's owner due to the severe halitosis that this location creates! The more infected skinfolds involved, the stronger the odor. However, since the dog is still growing, most practitioners will take a conservative medical approach to the condition until it is apparent that the dog has reached his maturity. If the condition is not resolved with growth or becomes very severe, plastic surgery to remove the affected excess skin is advisable. Obviously, surgical tacking together of skin folds in a dog with this condition is not recommended as it would only provide a fertile field for bacterial growth; thus facial or eyelid tacking for entropion would be contraindicated. In the adult Shar-Pei, while the skin folds are fewer, the head may still be subject to the condition. Total body dermatitis is typically found in the over-weight animal. Lactating females have been known to develop dermatitis between the mammary glands.

Treatment of either interdigital or total body dermatitis consists of first clipping away any hair from the site(s) and the immediate vicinity. A general bathing with benzoyl peroxide shampoo should follow. Many Shar-Pei breeders treat localized hot spots with an antiseptic solution that may be purchased from the veterinarian or homemade: it is a mixture of 5% boracic acid, 5% tannic acid, 5% salicylic acid, in 20% alcohol. (In some cases your vet will help devise the proper amounts of each substance that is best for the dog's specific skin problem.) Applied gently several times a day, it will help to dry the lesions. This solution does temporarily stain the skin; however, it has the added benefit that most dogs do not like the taste and will stop licking the area. Care must be taken with the dog who has open wounds, as the alcohol base would be very painful; in that case, a solution of Domeboro would be in order. A topical anti-inflammatory cream such as Vetalog should be applied as directed. Severe cases of pyoderma will require both topical and systemic antibiotics. Once the sites are healed, frequently dusting the areas with an antiseptic powder may discourage recurrence.

Many practitioners believe that the curative benefits of hydrotherapy should not be overlooked. A simple procedure for the owner, hydrotherapy may be incorporated into the dog's daily activities. Many owners simply place the animal into the bathtub and, with warm water, gently rinse the affected areas. Careful drying of the dog is important to prevent the moist skin from further trauma. Obviously, another measure that will alleviate the condition is weight reduction in the obese animal.

Since any irritation can initiate this skin response, care must also be taken to guard the animal from sunburn. In the Shar-Pei the hairs that cover a skin fold change direction as the skin curves. This allows the unprotected underlying skin to be directly exposed to the sun's rays. Just as the top of a balding head burns from the constant exposure, so to does the "top" of the Shar-Pei's wrinkles. Light-colored dogs are particularly prone, although even black dogs are subject. (See Hypopigmentation) Avoiding outdoor exposure at the peak of the day and shading dog runs will decrease the amount of exposure.

The prognosis for the dog depends on the ability to remove or improve the causative factors whether they be excess moisture, skin or other environmental factors.

HYPOPIGMENTATION

This skin condition refers to the absence of pigment, or color, in the coat or skin of the dog. It can be either congenital or acquired.

A true lack of skin pigment is called albinism and is passed as a rare hereditary trait. For some reason these animals have a lack of a certain enzyme vital for the production of melanin. This condition is typified by pure white coat hair, pink irises and pink-to-red nose and paw pads. This should not be confused with the white or cream form of coat color! These animals are extremely weather and light sensitive and should be carefully shielded. As a result, breeding of albino animals is strongly discouraged.

White or cream-colored dogs are subject to nasal solar dermatitis due to a lack of pigmentation on the broad, top surface of the nose. As the nose is inevitably exposed to the sun, the condition worsens until it can cover the entire nose surface. One theory is that the extremely fine and short hair, at the junction of the smooth nose tissue and the coat, allows for sunlight to penetrate to the epithelial level. (In other areas of coat, even among light-colored dogs, the longer, thicker body hair lie in a more horizontal position, shading the underlying skin.) In lighter animals this exposed area of the nose, frequently moistened by licking and nasal fluids, essentially becomes sun-burned. The skin will redden and peel repeatedly, never completely healing. Topical treatment is difficult due to the dog's propensity to lick off any medication. Some breeders have had limited success with frequently applying a maximum strength, human sun-block cream to the nose and adjoining fur.

In the Shar-Pei, the skin folds may also be subject to the same type of solar response. As the skin curves over the "wrinkle," the hairs are directed upward, exposing the skin. Sunburn in the cream and white Shar-Pei is particularly common. If the animal must be in direct sunlight for a prolonged period of time, or during peak sun hours, shading the

dog is recommended. Placing a T-shirt on the dog and securing it at the "waist" with masking tape will provide body wrinkles with temporary shade.

Another skin condition, common to the Chow Chow and the Shar-Pei, is due to a tyrosinase deficiency. The characteristic blue-black tongue turns pink and coat hairs turn white at the skin-shaft junction. In some cases the interior of the dog's mouth will lose all pigmentation. Most practitioners believe that this lack of tyrosinase is a genetic fault that appears during puppyhood. It is not believed to be an acquired disorder from external factors such as stress, nutritional deficiencies or weather changes. Since tyrosinase is necessary for the production of melanin, a skin biopsy can confirm the defect. At this time there is no treatment for the condition. In some animals, the disorder is self-limiting and resolves in two to four months.

Acquired depigmentation of the nose, lips and eyelids has been proposed to have an association with contact to plastic food and water dishes. Some dogs appear to be sensitive to the components of the plastic used in the bowl's manufacture. During the process of eating and drinking, they develop a dermatitis reaction to the material. Switching to glass or stainless steel dishes, bowls and buckets should initiate an immediate improvement in the condition. Use of these non-reactive materials must be continued throughout the dog's lifetime.

SHAR-PEI SYNDROME

Dr. George H. Muller, D.V.M. of the American College of Veterinary Dermatology, coined the name for this syndrome. The condition is characterized by a redness and inflammation of the underbody of the animal. Hair loss may be in a specific body area or in a more generalized pattern across the entire animal. Many of these dogs have a mottled appearance which Dr. Muller describes as "moth-eaten." Routine laboratory findings are normal. Once all other possible disorders have been excluded, then the Shar-Pei syndrome is considered. The exact cause is still unknown.

One theory is that, as in skinfold dermatitis, the short, bristly coat may be the cause, or at least be the instigator, of the problem. As the short hairs are folded back onto themselves, within the many folds of the Shar-Pei, they begin to rub and cause friction. The increased heat and irritation from the constant rubbing begins a reaction-response within the skin. As the rubbing continues, the body's response becomes more generalized, involving areas of skin not directly within the folds. This theory holds that the animal is reacting to the irritation of its own coat. (It is known that the Shar-Pei "horse" coat can cause a similar response in a sensitive human. These individuals develop raised red and/or itchy patches, especially of the forearm, when in direct contact with the Shar-Pei coat.) Whatever the cause, Dr. Muller has found that these animals do exhibit abnormally high amounts of imusin, a component in the dermis layer of their skin. What role this excessive amount plays in the condition is presently unclear.

For many practitioners and owners the diagnosis of Shar-Pei syndrome may come only after extensive, negative testing for multiple other disease entities. Some practitioners are not even convinced that this is a true disease state in itself, but may be only a conglomeration of other physical factors. Whatever the exact mechanism of the condition, it does not respond well to treatment of any variety. It is hopeful that within the next few years more information will be available.

INFANTILE PUSTULAR DERMATOSIS

Infantile Pustular Dermatosis has been recently acknowledged as a syndrome affecting the Chinese Shar-Pei, Labradors and Pointers. It begins suddenly between three days to three weeks of age. The puppies present with skin pustules which soon change to small yellow or pink round sores confined mostly to the head and trunk of the body. As these sores ooze, clumped mats of hair become trapped within the crusts. While pups may be active and afebrile, most are lethargic and have poor appetites. Within the same litter some pups may have few symptoms while others are severely ill. Lack of treatment of severe cases has resulted in death.

This puzzling disease appears not to be a bacterial infection as originally thought. Sterile culturing of the pustules indicate no presence of organisms. Regardless, most vets will prescribe systemic antibiotics to help the pup to fight off other organisms that may attack him in his weakened state. The antibiotic most commonly used is from the broad-spectrum cephalosporin drug family. This drug is effective against most gram-positive and some gram-negative bacteria, such as *E coli, Proteus, Klebsiella, Salmonella, Shigella* and *Pseudomonas*. It is relatively nontoxic.

Hydrotherapy is of major value in this condition. Placing the animal in a sink and gently rinsing the areas with warm water helps in the healing process. (A towel or rubber mat placed in the bottom of the sink will help the puppy feel secure.) This therapy should be repeated at least once a day with careful drying of the dog.

The young age of these animals makes diligent nursing care imperative. Bedding should be kept scrupulously clean and dry. Additional heat may be required if the pups are acutely ill. Supplemental hand feeding may be necessary. Should they become dehydrated, hospitalization may be required.

Treatment of the disease itself is with triamcinalone acetonide (Vetalog, Squibb, 2mg. per ml) at a dose of 0.1 mg. by injection, given once daily for a *maximum* of five days. Use of this drug leads to a positive prognosis. Recovery takes approximately one to two weeks. Relapses are possible but not common.

JUVENILE CELLULITIS

Juvenile cellulitis is also known by the names of juvenile pyoderma or "puppy strangles." It is a disease that confines itself to puppies of over three weeks but under four months of age.

Typically affecting short-coated breeds, it is found in the Shar-Pei, Dachshund, Golden Retriever and Pointer. As in Infantile pustular dermatosis, the disease runs the gamut from mild to acute severity, with pups within the same litter having varying degrees.

Lesions are typically found around the face and head, at junctions between mucous membranes and "exterior" skin, the ear, eyelid, anus and foreskin regions. The lesions do not contain bacterial organisms unless contaminated by licking or scratching. Puppies with milder cases may be alert and active, while severe cases present with fever, anorexia, and lethargy. The symptoms of painful, reddened, swollen, shiny skin, hair loss and oozing crusts may appear suddenly; lymph nodes in the head and throat are swollen. Lack of veterinary treatment has been known to lead to the death of the pup.

Systemic antibiotics are necessary to combat secondary bacterial organisms that may threaten the weakened pup. After antibiotic treatment has begun, triamcinalone or dexamethasone should follow. Hydrotherapy is important to the healing process. The pup should be placed into a bathtub for warm, gentle rinsing of the skin. A hand-held shower massager with gentle pressure is of invaluable help. Treating sites that are difficult to bathe, such as ears or the underside of the chin, can be treated by holding soaks of Domeboro's solution to the area three to four times a day for at least five minutes. The pup should be carefully dried and placed in a warm, dry, clean bed. After the hydrotherapy, topical ointments may be effectively applied. Severely ill pups should be given close supervision and hospitalization if necessary.

The response to treatment is encouraging and usually begins within four to five days. With prompt attention, scarring of the skin may be the only lasting effect of this condition.

Thriving, alert puppies. Yao'Shu's Cloisonne X Da Hei Xiong puppies. Margery Denton, photo.

CHAPTER FOUR

ENDOCRINE AND IMMUNE DISORDERS

HYPOTHYROIDISM

In the dog, two small thyroid glands are found on either side of the trachea or windpipe. They are present and active at birth and continue to play an important life-long part in the physiological functioning of the animal. Puppies born with absent or non-functioning thyroid glands do not survive.

The thyroid glands produce hormones, T_3 and T_4, which affect the metabolism of the animal's entire system, from the smallest cell to the most complex physical interaction. T_4, also called thyroxine, is the major hormone produced. Its production is triggered by the hypothalamus, a tiny organ in the brain, which secretes TRH, or thyrotropin-releasing hormone. TRH is delivered to the pituitary gland where it signals the need for another hormone, TSH or thyroid-stimulating hormone, to be released. TSH is then carried to the thyroid glands by way of the blood stream. Its arrival causes the release of T_4 and its later conversion to T_3, also known as tri-iodothyronine. T_3 is the most potent form of the thyroid hormones and is directly responsible for the gland's effect on the body. Small amounts of these hormones are stored within the thyroid gland itself. However, as the body depletes its supply of these hormones, their level in the blood decreases. The hypothalamus senses the decrease in hormone levels and the process is started over again by the release of TRH.

The thyroid hormones can be compared to a multi-talented supervisor who monitors, regulates and participates in the functioning of the cells. The thyroid hormones are responsible for the utilization of oxygen at the cell level and the over-all metabolic rate of the animal. In order to do this, the hormones combine their actions with other hormones or enzymes to breakdown and use protein, fat and carbohydrates ingested by the dog. As a result, they affect growth and development, reproduction, and skin integrity. In fact, there are very few physical components of the dog that are not influenced by thyroid secretions. Thus, the ramifications of defects within this hypothalamus-pituitary-thyroid complex are staggering.

Most disorders originate in the thyroid gland itself, although they can occasionally stem from deeper problems in the hypothalamus or pituitary. In any case, the ultimate consequence is a decrease in the amount of circulating T_3 and its resulting physiological impact. Hypothyroidism refers to a disorder of the production of these thyroid hormones resulting in the circulation of lower than optimal levels.

Hypothyroidism is classically demonstrated by middle-aged animals of between four and six years of age. Large or giant breeds tend to develop the condition at an earlier age. It does not appear to be sex-related, although there may be a breed-related predisposition. A higher than normal incidence of hypothyroidism is found in the Boxer, Dachshund, Doberman Pinscher, Golden Retriever, Great Dane, Irish Setter, Miniature Schnauzer and Poodle. Other breeds that are beginning to show an increased incidence are the Afghan Hound, Airedale, Bulldog, Chow Chow, Cocker Spaniel, Irish Wolfhound, Malamute, Newfoundland, Pomeranian, Shetland Sheepdog and Shar-Pei.

The onset is usually gradual, with the signs and symptoms frequently being accepted by the owner as a part of the aging process. The dogs become increasingly obese although the appetite remains the same. Their physical and mental activity level rapidly declines with more and more time spent sleeping. They seek out the warmest spot in their environment, sometimes following the sun from window to window. Sexual interest is suppressed. Females have difficulty conceiving or maintaining a pregnancy. Low-grade anemia is common.

Skin and coat changes are an important symptom of the disorder. Loss of coat occurs on the nose, tail, sides, ears, hind legs, lower abdomen and armpits. As more hair follicles fail to replace the lost hair, the condition gradually spreads. Classically, hypothyroidism has non-itchy, bilaterally symetrical hair loss. This change in appearance is typically what the owner first notices. Some skin areas begin to form the darkened scales of seborrhea. Lesions are most often found on pressure points, armpits and forelegs. (See Seborrhea) The skin begins to thicken, called myxedema or "elephant skin," and takes on a roughened, exaggerated, saggy appearance particularly around the head and neck. Ear canals may become chronically inflamed. Research supports the theory that hypothyroidism decreases the dog's resistance to infection and allows the

Skin disorders stemming from hypothyroidism.

chronic, severe, resistant pyodermas often found.

Thyroid deficiency has also been theoretically associated with the fading puppy syndrome. This exhibits itself within days, even hours, after birth. The puppies are at first active and healthy, then suddenly they begin to fail, with death resulting within the first week of life. Quite often the dam when tested is found to have low thyroid levels, although she may or may not as yet have outward symptoms of the disorder. Apparently the puppies are either adversely affected in utero by the dam's metabolic disorder or their thyroids failed to function adequately after birth.

Diagnosis of hypothyroidism is dependent on clinical examination and positive laboratory results. By running a blood test for the levels of both T_3 and T_4, an accurate picture of the dog's thyroid function is available. Tests need to be handled by a laboratory that is prepared for the smaller amount of these hormones found in dog's blood; use of a human's laboratory produces results that are misleading. The current theory is that lowered levels of either or both thyroid hormones indicates that further testing should be conducted.

Within the past two years, newer tests have been developed that can determine not only the levels of T_3 and T_4 but of TSH and TRH as well. These methods, called TSH and TRH assay tests and TSH and TRH stimulation tests, can distinguish between problems originating in the thyroid gland or in the brain. The stimulation tests function on the concept that if the problem is thyroid gland related, no amount of additional TSH or TRH will increase the circulating thyroid hormones. If, however, the disorder originates in the hypothalamus, then additional TRH injected into the dog will result in increased levels of circulating thyroid hormones. Similarly, if the problem is in the pituitary, additional TSH will cause increased circulating thyroid hormones.

In very rare circumstances, some dogs will test normal in all of the usual tests yet will display symptoms of the disease. It has been found that some animals have an underlying protein metabolic disorder of the intestinal tract and develop a form of hypothyroidism. In these animals the problem arises from the inability to absorb and utilize protein from the food they ingest. This malabsorption in turn creates a protein deficiency so that the thyroid hormones, which "travel" in the blood connected to protein molecules, have no means of transportation. The animal exhibits the physical signs of traditional hypothyroidism even though the pituitary, hypothalamus and thyroids are all functioning properly. Treatment of this form of pseudo-hypothyroidism focuses on reversal of the intestinal problem. (See Malabsorption)

Other factors that may incorrectly influence hypothyroid test results are: age, breed, time of day, weight, food intake, other current illnesses, steroid medications, and pregnancy. Many practitioners carefully schedule the time the initial diagnostic blood screening test is taken. Any abnormal environmental influences should be carefully avoided.

Treatment of hypothyroidism consists of thyroid hormone replacement for the remainder of the animal's life since in most cases hypothyroidism is a life-long disorder. Daily drug therapy will always be required. Actual animal hormone extracts are available to treat the condition. One disadvantage of any animal hormone derivative is that the concentration of the chemical may vary from pill to pill. Exact quality control, to insure the same dose in every pill is not possible, due to the variation in the source of the substance. Furthermore,

the use of generic thyroid hormone drugs has not been successful; while many generic drugs can be utilized in the treatment of various medical conditions, the use of generic hormones does not always meet with a curative response.

To try to counter these problems, synthetic varieties of these hormones have been used in the past few years. Sodium levothyroxine, or T4, is most commonly used and is given once or twice a day. If the dog fails to respond to the T_4 replacement, liothyronine may be given. It is essentially a T_3 preparation and is given either two or three times a day. Ideally, these synthetic forms have the advantages of the naturally occurring form and would modify its disadvantages due to the ability to control its manufacture.

Although hormone replacement is not an expensive drug regime, the animal will need to be occasionally tested to

CLINICAL SIGNS OF HYPOTHYROIDISM

METABOLIC

listlessness	weakness
dull mental status	difficulty walking
exercise intolerance	weight gain
normal appetite	sensitivity to cold

REPRODUCTION

infertility	long intervals between cycles
prolonged cycle bleeding	fading puppies
lack of sexual drive	testicular atrophy

SKIN CHANGES

dry, scaly skin	increased skin pigmentation
brittle hair	seborrhea
loss of hair	myxedema
skin infections	

SYSTEMIC

slowing of the heart rate	diarrhea
irregular heart beat	vomiting
fat deposits in the cornea of the eye	uveitis/corneal ulcerations
depression of immune system	

determine that the dosage is appropriate. These blood monitoring tests involve taking a blood sample to determine the lowest level of circulating hormone. Some practitioners believe that, for animals receiving the drug twice a day, this blood test should be done immediately before, and six hours after, pill administration; however, if the animal is receiving the drug only once a day, the blood sample should be taken just prior to the pill being given and then retested eight hours later. Either approach requires that the owner make sure that the appointment with the veterinarian is scheduled at the proper time! Delays of even a few hours can dramatically alter the test results and may ultimately lead to improper treatment. These tests are repeated every two weeks until the dog is stabilized and then again every 6-12 months over his lifetime.

A dog's response to the replacement therapy typically has stages. Within one week, the animal may respond to the drug by improvement in his activity and mental status. Within a couple of weeks weight loss begins as the body stabilizes its metabolism. The final stage may come four to six weeks later as the follicles on the trunk and tail slowly replace the hair. In some cases, however, especially on the ears, the hair may never return.

Treatment failure is uncommon. It is typically caused by failure of the owner to continue the medication on schedule, failure of the dog to actually swallow the pill, faulty assimilation into the body, or an error in diagnosis. Should the dog fail to respond to treatment, a review of the medical history would be in order.

Fortunately, hypothyroidism, once diagnosed, is readily treated. The prognosis for the vast majority of dogs with this disorder is a normal, active life.

ADDISON'S DISEASE

Canine adrenal hormone production is a complicated feed-back system involving the interaction of the brain, blood and adrenal glands. It begins in the brain's hypothalamus organ where the primary control of the series of steps, eventually triggering adrenal hormonal action, is seated. The hypothalamus secretes a hormone called the corticotropin-releasing factor, or CRF, which when carried to the pituitary, signals it to release another hormone, ACTH. ACTH, or adrenocorticotropic hormone, is then in turn carried by the blood to the adrenal glands which are located near the two kidneys. These adrenal glands are responsible for the secretion of a number of hormones which impact a multitude of body systems. As the amount of circulating adrenal hormones decreases, that information is fed back to the brain's hypothalamus where the cycle begins again.

The adrenal glands themselves are divided into an outer portion, called the cortex, and an inner core, called the medulla. Although the same organ, the two divisions function almost as if they are separate structures. The inner medulla section of the adrenal gland is the primary source of epinephrine (adrenalin) and its related substances. While important in crisis situations, epinephrine is not critical for life. The outer cortex segment is divided into three layers which are responsible for the production of mineralocorticoids, glucocorticoids and some sex hormones, respectively. These first two are so essential that to be without them threatens survival.

The most important glucocorticoids manufactured by the cortex are cortisol (hydrocortisone) and corticosterone. The two glucocorticoids influence almost every cell and system in the body: they promote normal protein, carbohydrate and fat breakdown into glucose, help the body to cope with stress, and maintain normal blood pressure. They also have an anti-inflammatory action by maintaining capillary and interior cellular stability.

The mineralocorticoids are composed of aldosterone and desoxycorticosterone. Their primary function is to reabsorb sodium and chloride and excrete potassium from within the kidney tubules. This impact on the conservation of sodium by the kidneys thereby directly influences water retention in the body. Cardiac output and arterial pressure are also under the influence of these substances. The proper circulation of the total-body blood volume depends on these functions. Finally, mineralocorticoids potentiates the body's inflammatory response to injury.

Thus, a defect in the structure or function of the adrenal cortex would have a disastrous impact on the dog's physical well-being. Addison's disease, or hypoadrenocorticism, refers primarily to a decreased circulating blood level of the mineralo- and glucocorticoids which results in a broad complex of physical symptoms and conditions.

Because of their interconnectedness, a disorder in any of the three major organ centers of the adrenal complex, hypothalamus, pituitary or adrenal gland, may cause an adrenal hormone deficit. Most frequently a decrease in the amount of circulating glucocorticoids and mineralocorticoids indicates a dysfunction of actual adrenal gland tissue due to an idiopathic response, lesion, tumor, hemorrhage, infarction, drug over-dose or autoimmune disease. In these cases an extensive destruction of the adrenal glands must have occurred in order for overt clinical signs to be present. Most research indicates that destruction of a staggering 90% or more of the adrenal tissue is required before the animal begins to display symptoms. However, damage to the brain's hypothalamus or pituitary can also cause decreased hormonal production and circulation by failing to "switch on" the adrenals. In either case, the animal's physical status is in jeopardy.

The clinical signs of Addison's disease reflect the scope of the glands' functions: weight loss, poor appetite, depressed mental state, muscular weakness, exercise intolerance, trembling, vomiting, diarrhea, thirst, abdominal tenderness, subnormal body temperature, poor capillary refill, hypotension and bradycardia. The typical dog is less than six years old and female. No direct breed relationship has been proven; however, some breeds like the Shar-Pei may be prone to this disorder.

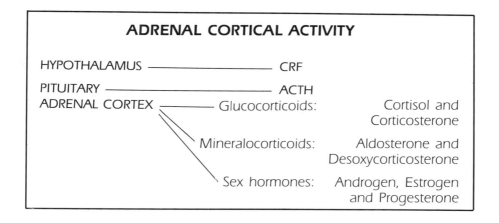

ADRENAL CORTICAL ACTIVITY

HYPOTHALAMUS ——————————— CRF

PITUITARY ————————————— ACTH

ADRENAL CORTEX ————— Glucocorticoids: Cortisol and Corticosterone

Mineralocorticoids: Aldosterone and Desoxycorticosterone

Sex hormones: Androgen, Estrogen and Progesterone

While the underlying condition is always present, an acute phase can surface suddenly. Undue stress is the initiating factor in the acute response. Stress can rapidly change a chronic condition into an acute emergency called adrenal crisis, with resulting hypovolemic shock, cardiac failure and death, if treatment is not instituted. This intolerance to stress is the fundamental physiological defect of Addison's disease. The animal's system is already severely compromised by a deficit adrenal hormonal level, making any additional stress physically devastating.

While not an emotional disorder, Addisonian animals are particularly vulnerable to stress since they have less emotional and physical flexibility. Stress, as perceived by some dogs, can be as overt as an injury by another animal or as subtle as rearrangement of the home's furniture. A trip to the vet, moving, or even a feared vacuum cleaner can over-tax the animal's struggling coping mechanism. The event, although seemingly insignificant, is the final straw that throws the animal into a full-blown adrenal crisis. Similarly, a crisis-trigger can be either a major or minor physical illness which is perceived by the body as stress and therefore is life-threatening. It is the dog's agitated emotional/physical response to the situation that overloads his physical reserves. *Any* change that the dog is not used to can trigger a crisis response.

In acute adrenal crisis, the animal must first be stabilized before diagnosis or treatment can begin. The animal must be given aggressive medical intervention to counteract the effects of the cardiovascular collapse: the animal is hospitalized for treatment of shock. Intravenous solutions are begun to replace the missing electrolytes and circulating blood volume. Once the animal is stable, then treatment of the underlying disease can begin.

Diagnosis of Addison's disease depends on overt clinical signs and positive laboratory findings. The most important lab test available for diagnosis is the ACTH response test. It determines the current functioning level of the adrenal glands. A blood sample is taken which indicates the normal, baseline level of naturally circulating adrenal hormones. An injection of ACTH is given to the animal to stimulate adrenal hormone secretion. Two hours later, a second blood sample is obtained to determine the response to the injected hormone. If the response level is low, it can be assumed that the adrenal glands can no longer produce their required amounts of adrenal hormones. Replacement hormone therapy will be necessary.

Replacement therapy is successfully accomplished by a daily, oral dose of Florinef. The exact dose is determined by each individual animal's needs and involves a repeated blood test approximately seven days after discharge from the hospital. Once the proper dosage amount is determined, the blood is rechecked every four to six months during the first year, and annually thereafter. In addition, $\frac{1}{2}$ to 2 grams of table salt will need to be added to the daily food intake. This increase in sodium will help to conserve the water and electrolytes necessary for proper circulatory functioning.

Home care of the Addisonian animal requires an attentive owner who must be aware of the animal's limitations. The animal must be protected from any unnecessary stress, which will depend on the individual dog. In unavoidable situations, such as visits to the vet, an increase in the dosage of supplemental glucocorticoids, according to the vet's instructions, will help the animal to compensate.

In general, these animals respond well to replacement hormone treatment. Although the owner must be forever protectively vigilant, the dog can enjoy a healthy and active life.

IgA IMMUNE DEFICIENCY IN THE SHAR-PEI

The dog's overall immune system is a highly complex defense system. Its intricate role in the well-being of the animal cannot be over-stated. It is the major source of the body's protection and is still not completely understood. Research into its interactions continues. In order to best understand the function of its broad range of components, at the risk of over-simplification, it can best be compared to an ivy-league school having two top-ranked athletic teams.

The respective teams play their own sport by their own rules within the larger framework of the school's playing field. Although they function somewhat independently of the rest of the student body, their primary goal is to win and thereby preserve the reputation of the school and its students. On each team is an assortment of players who have their own assigned positions and specialized roles while still functioning as a greater unit, the team. Each team may have a first and second string of players who are put into the game as required. In a well-coordinated team, the skill of each player contributes to the ultimate success of the whole. Occasionally there may be a talented player or two who, in an emergency, can play on either team to fill in as the need arises.

The dog's immune system is organized very similarly to this hypothetical school athletic team. While there exist many methods of classifying the basic players within the immune system, the most direct method divides it into two basic immune response types, called the humoral and the cell-mediated. The humoral "team" refers to the response elements in the serum, plasma or blood, and cell-mediated refers to the response centering around specialized cellular structures. Both divisions serve to successfully meet any "team" (organism or substance) that challenges the body. The ultimate victory insures the well-being of the body, or the "school." Within each of these two immune teams is a variety of "players" that have their own specialized functions.

The first team, the humoral system, is composed mostly of antibodies, a form of protein molecule called an immunoglobulin, which are free-floating in the plasma or blood serum. There are five major immunoglobulins: G, A, M, D, and E, which have their own assigned tasks. Their role is to neutralize toxins, penetrate an offending organism's external membrane, and respond defensively to the reappearance of a foreign substance. The typical allergic responses are examples of the humoral system at work. (See Allergies) Defects in the hu-

---

THE IMMUNE SYSTEM

Humoral:
- antibody—5 classes of immunoglobulin proteins; G,A,M,D,E
- each class has own function
- appears on second exposure; immediate response

Cell-Mediated:
- produces effector molecules which transfers cells, inhibits migration of cells, initiates cell destruction, generates hypersensitivity response, coordinates uncommitted cells, produces Interferon for viral infections
- appears on second exposure but response is delayed 24–48 hours

Immunodeficiencies

Disease	Breed
Primary (congenital):	
Canine cyclic hematopoiesis	Collie
Canine granulocytopathy syndrome	Irish Setter
Neutrophil bactericidal defect	Doberman pinscher
Pelger-Huet anomaly	various breeds
Complement deficiency	Brittany spaniel
Selective IgM deficiency	Doberman pinscher
Selective IgA deficiency	German Shepherd, beagle, Shar-Pei
Transient hypogammaglobulinemia	Samoyed
Combined immunodeficiency disease	Basset hound
Immunodeficient dwarfism	Weimaraner

Secondary (acquired):
Infectious—distemper, parvovirus, demodicosis, fungal infections
Drug induced—glucocorticoids, cytotoxic agents, anesthetic agents, antibiotics, estrogens, phenylbutazone
Toxins—heavy metals, phenolics, herbicides, enterotoxins
Nutritional—calorie deficit, protein deficit, vitamin or mineral deficit, caloric excess
Endocrine—hyperadrenocorticism, diabetes, pregnancy, hyperestrogenism
Miscellaneous—removal of spleen, tumor, trauma, renal disease, maternal-milk deprivation

moral system are common in man and are the type of immune deficit most frequently found in the Shar-Pei.

The second team, the cell-mediated system, is composed of a variety of lymphocytes which produce effector molecules, whose role comprise a wide range of defensive mechanisms. They are responsible for the mobilization of the body's organic defenses, congregation of certain defensive cells, direction of cell destruction, physical alteration or destruction of foreign substances, and manufacture of certain substances to battle specific organisms, i.e. Interferon and its actions against viruses. In addition they are responsible for what is known as a delayed-reaction response such as occurs with some types of contact dermatitis, i.e. the body does not display its response until 24-48 hours after a second exposure. Finally, they can call in "uncommitted" defense cells should the body require it.

Defects of the immunological system have far-reaching implications for the health and survival of the dog. Primary defects are those rare congenital abnormalities that are present from birth and predispose the dog to disease entities. Secondary defects in the immune system are considered to be acquired, since they are not present at birth and are generated from an external source such as drugs, diseases, toxins, nutritional imbalances, endocrine disorders, and miscellaneous other factors. These conditions can additionally create a favorable environment for other opportunistic infections.

Secondary defects occur when initial humoral immunity is not obtained by the normal method: initial humoral immunity should be obtained by the passive transfer of the mother's antibodies to her offspring. As the puppies nurse during the first hours of milk production, they acquire this protection until their own immature immune systems can protect them. Unfortunately, the mother's immunity does not last. Therefore, the process of passively acquired immunity from the dam must be assisted by inoculations from the veterinarian, thereby providing the stimulus for the puppy's own immune system to produce defenses against the major canine diseases. Without it, these diseases are the major cause of death due to the neonatal animal's immune deficiency.

An immune deficiency could also be generated as a secondary response to another disease entity. Viral infections such as parvovirus and distemper can cause an IgA deficit. Fulminating skin infections such as demodex and some fungi have been associated with this disorder. (See Demodicosis)

Certain drugs, including the glucocorticoids, can suppress the body's normal immune status. (See Addison's disease) Antibiotics and anesthetics have been documented as decreasing immune molecules produced by certain cells in the body; chloramphenicol, dapsone, sulfamethoxypyridazine, clindamycin, lincomycin, and griseofulvin have all been suspect. In addition, estrogens have been linked with an impairment in the immune system. This factor could have major implications for Shar-Pei breeders! Environmental toxins can also cause immune deficits. Lead, cadmium, mercury, zinc, cobalt, nickel, carbon dust, silicon dioxide, arsenical, PCB, PBB, and DDT are some of the offending toxins.

The nutritional status of the animal has been implicated in secondary conditions. Loss of protein, overwhelming parasites, inadequate diet, or severe appetite abnormalities are major factors in immuno-defects. A deficiency in almost any of the various vitamins or minerals can be a suppressive factor. Conversely, excesses of vitamin A, C, iron or zinc have been connected with immune imbalance. The difficulty in providing adequate nutrition was clearly shown in a study that researched the dietary requirements of various disease states: dogs with fractures required a 10-30% increase in protein and calories; dogs with infections needed a 20-60% increase in calories; and dogs with burns required a 60-100% increase in calories! Obviously, proper nutrition is of major importance in the health of the dog, seemingly minor imbalances perhaps leading to a nutritional immunodeficiency. For this reason, any changes in a dog's dietary intake should always be made with a veterinarian's assistance.

Finally, endocrine alterations can cause a secondary immune deficiency. Cushing's syndrome, diabetes, and hyperestrogenism can influence the level of available immune defense. Pregnancy, while not a disease state, purposefully causes a decrease in the body's reaction to foreign substances in order to protect the developing fetus. (This is the only situation where a relative immune deficiency is desirable!)

The most commonly seen primary disorder of the immunoglobins is the selective IgA deficiency. This is the disorder most recognized in the Shar-Pei. It is believed that a deficit in this particular immunoglobulin results in an increased susceptibility to disease. The role of IgA is fundamental to the control of viral infections within the respiratory, intestinal, and urinary tracts. It also functions to inhibit the absorption of antigens from the internal mucosal linings. IgA deficiency in both man and dog create similar symptoms: upper respiratory infections, otitis media, opportunistic skin infections, gastrointestinal upsets, allergies, and other immune abnormalities. While IgA deficiency is well documented in man, the exact cause of a primary condition has not been determined; however, defects in the humoral system of the Shar-Pei, specifically an IgA deficit, are considered congenital and highly familial. In one study done by Moroff, Hurvitz, Peterson, Saunders, and Noone at the Animal Medical Center in New York City, the mating of two affected animals produced five puppies of which four had an IgA deficiency.

In this same study of Shar-Pei, an IgA deficiency involved sinus, respiratory, and skin disorders: the affected dogs had pulmonary congestion, cough, nasal discharge, conjunctivitis, otitis media, fever, demodex, and an atopy-like skin rash. (See Atopy; Demodex) In addition, normally harmless bacteria were allowed to over-proliferate and cause disease. This complex of symptoms is only logical if the function of IgA is considered; a breakdown in the mucosal protection within these areas would open the door to foreign organisms and antigens.

Furthermore, in this same study, it was discovered that the normal Shar-Pei were 76.9% lower in their IgA levels than other normal dogs. This strongly supports a breed predisposition. One theory has proposed that a combination of genetic defects must be present in order to cause clinical symptoms of a IgA deficiency. However, this important distinction still needs to be clarified: whether the IgA deficit in the Shar-Pei is a primary condition or secondary to another entity. In fact, it has been proven in man that merely having a lowered IgA level does not definitely mean a disease state, since other defensive "team members" are at work. Thus, a lowered IgA level does not necessarily mean a disease is present or inevitable!

It has been suggested that testing serum IgA levels at 16 weeks of age could detect an IgA deficiency. Thus, if it is confirmed that Shar-Pei are vulnerable to disease with a lowered IgA, it may be possible to predetermine if a potential breeding animal has a primary defect. Research into this concept is continuing.

Cure of a primary IgA disorder is currently not available. In secondary IgA deficiencies, however, treatment or removal of the causative factor(s) may allow the return to normal IgA levels.

CHAPTER FIVE

ORTHOPEDIC DISORDERS

HIP DYSPLASIA

Canine Hip Dysplasia is not a new phenomenon; it has even been found in the remains of cave man's pre-domesticated dog. What is new, since 1935 when hip dysplasia was first officially reported, is the interest in and study of the condition. Hip dysplasia was one of the first structural diseases to be connected to a genetic cause. Research continues in an attempt to eradicate this leading crippler of the present-day dog. Few contemporary breeds are immune to this condition. Once thought to be prevalent only in the large or giant breeds, today researchers realize that breeds as light and nimble as the Cocker Spaniel and the Shetland Sheepdog are also prone. Entire organizations have been created to spearhead research and collection of data. It is one disease that unites researchers, dog registries, breeders and pet owners world wide.

The hip is actually a complex meeting of multiple, specialized bone surfaces, creating what is called a "ball-and-socket" joint. The top of the dog's leg bone, called the femur head, is rounded into the shape of a smooth ball. This shape facilitates the rotating and angular movements required by the dog's hind legs. The femur head fits snugly into a cup-like cavity, called the acetabulum, at the lower outside edges of the boney pelvic structure. The indented shape of the cup provides stability to the joint,

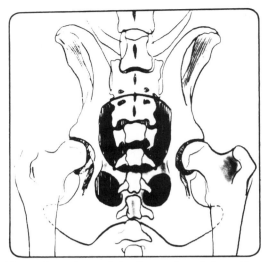

Normal canine pelvis. Reproduced from Radiographic Interpretation for the Small Animal Clinician *by Jerry M. Owens, D.V.M.; Darryl N. Biery, D.V.M., Consulting Editor.*

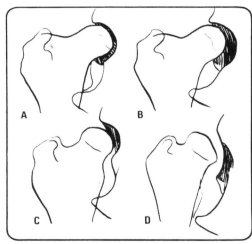

Canine Hip Displasia. The normal hip is seen in A. Sublux ation is present in B. In C, the acetabulum is shallow and subluxation is present. In D, luxation is present with femoral head flattening. Reproduced from Radiographic Interpretation for the Small Animal Clinician *by Jerry M. Owens, D.V.M.; Darryl N. Biery, D.V.M., Consulting Editor.*

keeping the head in place as the leg muscles move the limb back and forth. Since the dog's rear leg muscles are very powerful, the hip joint must be able to sustain the tremendous force applied as the dog runs, jumps and leaps. Proper formation and alignment of these bones are crucial to the dog's movement and mobility.

The term "dysplasia" refers to an abnormal development within the hip joint. The abnormality may be confined to a single aspect of one bone or to the multi-faceted interaction of their fit. For example, the head of the femur may be misshapen, or the socket may be too shallow, preventing the femur from seating itself properly. The socket may be too wide, allowing the ball to slip out of the space, or a combination of small defects in more than one bone may add up to a much larger problem. Whatever the structural error(s), the result is a separation of the femur head from the pelvic "girdle." This faulty space allows undue stress to be applied to the joint's surfaces as the dog goes about his daily activities. The body tries to compensate for the problem by increasing bone size, altering the shape of the cup or by muscular compensation. However, over time these efforts are ineffective in normalizing the integrity of the hip; the joint begins to deteriorate and degenerative joint disease ensues.

As in most physical conditions, there are levels and degrees of severity. In milder cases the only defect might be a laxity in the joint, causing few signs or symptoms. In moderate cases, the pup has little discomfort in its early development but then, between four and six months, may suddenly become lame. He may have an unsteady gait and/or hop with both hind legs held closely together. Climbing stairs or rising from a lying position may be difficult. Handling of the joint may be painful and cause the animal to cry out or snap. The owner frequently blames the lameness on over-exertion, jumping or climbing off or onto an object. The lameness usually resolves on its own, reinforcing the owner's "accident" theory. Most of these pups are pain-free, and even symptom-free, by eleven to thirteen months of age. Although the signs disappear, later in life these dogs will develop osteoarthritis, a progressive degenerative disease of the joint. In more severe cases, the animal may be gravely crippled at as early as six to twelve months of age.

Although, strictly speaking, hip dysplasia is not congenital, in that it is not obvious at birth, the hip's future has been genetically programmed. Furthermore, research indicates that dysplasia is polygenic in that the condition is an expression of multiple genes. It is only logical when the complexity of the ball-and-socket joint is considered. Each component of the joint, its shape, structure and muscle mass, are all independent elements. The exact number of genes or their exact interaction involved in the development of the hip joint is not known. As a result, it is impossible to breed for an improvement in one specific part of the joint. The hip must be viewed as an integrated whole whenever heredity is considered.

While the genetic basis of the condition cannot be denied, most researchers believe that there is also a variant that influences whether or not a dog will be clinically symptomatic. An odd facet of hip dysplasia is that the clinical picture may not be in line with the severity of the joint abnormality. Many animals with acutely dysplastic hips may compensate so well that, to the observer, they appear to be completely normal. In addition, the presence or absence of signs and symptoms, regardless of the degree of involvement, are very individualistic to the particular dog, his hip structure, and even his personality.

Most studies indicate that there may also be a strong environmental component to hip dysplasia. While the dog may carry the genetic tendency for the condition, the presence or absence of environmental factors may determine the degree of that particular dog's clinical response. Certain environmental influences may be of major significance as to whether the dysplasia has a functional impact. Environmental factors implicated in hip dysplasia include proper weight control, appropriate feeding practices of the young pup, and controlled exercise.

A factor implicated is the continual over-feeding of the growing pup. It has been found that the voracious over-eater of a litter may well be the one that eventually demonstrates hip dysplasia. Gross over-feeding appears to throw off the normal, coordinated process of muscle and bone growth, so that bones and joints, in particular, are required to support weight beyond their capabilities. The pups typically are sway-backed, have misshapen knees, and have rear feet that point in an east-west direction. Keeping the feeding schedule to the appropriate amount for that pup's age and size may well modify the occurrence of dysplasia. Obviously, even a normally formed joint will suffer damage if undue pressure is consistently present.

Another environmental factor that is directly related to the owner is the role of nutrition. It has been proven that the proper balance of calcium, phosphorus and Vitamin D is crucial to the correct development of bone, including the hip joint. Deficiency or excess in one or more of these elements will cause difficulties in the formation of healthy bones and joints. However, in most cases, the difficulty arises not with deficiencies, but with the over-supplementation of the dog's feed. Most evidence now indicates that a quality, complete dog food, wet or dry, supplies all the necessary required levels of these minerals. With over-supplementation, what would have been normal bone growth may actually be distorted. Additives of any sort should be first approved by the veterinarian before administration.

The appropriate exercise of a maturing pup is becoming more apparent as research into dysplasia continues. In the susceptible dog, the belief is that improper exercise or over-exercise during the early years may cause hip joint defects. As a result, many dog trainers are beginning to restrict high impact actions such as hurdle jumping, frisbee catching or other activities that require the hip to withstand tremendous impact in dogs under two years of age. Some discussion is presently underway as to the consequences of frequently running a young dog on cement or asphalt roadways. Just as the field of study of joint development in the young human athlete is in its infancy, so it is in the young dog. Conservative researchers are encouraging the reduction of high impact activities to allow the moldable joint to mature in a more normal fashion.

Other theories have been proposed that connect sex and/or growth factors to the development of dysplasia. Hormonal influence is involved in the growth and development of both bone and muscle structure of the maturing dog. The hormonal impact at a crucial age may predispose that animal to overt clinical signs. Other researchers have questioned whether dysplasia is, for some reason, a growth defect allowing the leg's muscle mass to grow out of synchronization with the bone development. This discrepancy would allow uneven stress to be applied to certain vulnerable aspects of the joint. Still other researchers suggest that there may be a larger medical condition at work and that hip dysplasia is just one of other affected joints.

Therefore, considering genetics and environment, there are three basic possibilities for hip dysplasia:

- bad genes and bad environment
  → overt hip dysplasia
- good genes and bad environment
  → overt and concealed hip dysplasia
- bad genes and good environment
  → overt or concealed hip dysplasia
- good genes and good environment
  → normal hips

Clinical symptoms, then, of an already dysplastic hip have variables, and their display may or may not be readily apparent.

Accurate diagnosis of hip dysplasia can only be made by radiography. In the past physical palpation was used to assess the condition of the hip. Unfortunately, follow-up studies later proved that hips that had been considered clear of dysplasia by palpation, when X-rayed, were found to be dysplastic. The differences in breed joint construction, breed muscle mass, the individual dog's cooperation and the experience of the practitioner make palpation unreliable. At present palpation continues to be used in conjunction with radiography in determining the dog's status. Palpation is useful in evaluating the very young pup that is being considered for a show or breeding career. If palpation is done during the early weeks, then preliminary X-raying may be delayed until the sixth month.

Radiographs may be taken by the owner's veterinary clinic. From these X-rays the practitioner will be able to give a diagnosis of the status of the hip. For the serious breeder or owners who intend to show their animals, further evaluation can be done by the Orthopedic Foundation for Animals Inc.(OFA), a central hip registry and diagnostic center for American purebred dog breeds. The X-ray is sent to the OFA, who has three certified veterinary radiologists independently review the films and render an opinion, for a small charge. These radiologists assign a classification to the hip joint based on the presence or absence of dysplasia: excellent, good, fair or borderline, or mild, moderate, or severe dysplasia. Those hips rating an excellent, good or fair category will be assigned a OFA registry number that is permanently affixed to the dog's official name. Borderline hips are considered questionable and require a second X-ray to be submitted in six to eight months. If then acceptable, a number can be assigned. Hips at any level of dysplasia are not given a registration number. Each breed's X-rays are considered in relation to those of other dogs of the same age, size and breed. The OFA will only accept X-rays of animals two years of age or older since the majority of the bone and muscle growth has been completed by that age. Preliminary films can be read by the OFA on a dog younger than two years, if that dog is intended for breeding or for competition, but a final review at two years will be required.

The X-raying procedure for hip dysplasia involves bringing the dog for its scheduled appointment. Since general anesthesia or sedation is usually required, the animal should not be fed or given water at least six hours prior to the procedure. These medications are required in order to keep the animal still while the back legs are arranged in the proper position for seeing the "interior outline" of the joint. With dogs that are relaxed and cooperative, some practitioners are striving to use minimal drugs during the procedure.

The dog is placed on his back with the rear legs fully extended and rotated inward. This allows the head of the femur to settle into its closest position to the pelvic cup. In dysplastic joints, the bones are misaligned, allowing a visible gap between the femur head and the acetabulum. The more dysplastic the joint, the more out of alignment and the larger the gap. If 50% of the femur head is not "covered" by, or in proximity to, the cup, the joint is considered to be dysplastic. In extreme cases, the head of the femur may be completely out of the acetabulum, a condition called luxation. This is the most severe of dysplastic conditions.

There are some situations where a false subluxation may be seen on X-ray. For this reason, the OFA does not recommend that films be taken if a female is in season. Apparently the increase in hormonal levels during a bitch's heat could cause a temporary relaxation of the hip's supporting structure, causing a dysplasia-like condition. They also recommend that dogs of either sex should not be X-rayed after long episodes of restricted activity, such as during hospitalization or kenneling. The resulting loss of muscle tone due to the lack of exercise could cause a pseudo-dysplasia that will resolve as normal activity is resumed. Contrary to popular belief, anesthesia does not cause false readings. During the procedure, the animal is only lightly anesthetized so that it does not affect the hip alignment. In fact, some research has indicated that the lack of anesthesia or sedation may cause faulty readings as the animal actively compensates during the procedure.

X-rays sent to the OFA must contain accurate information and identification. The film emulsion should contain the registered name of the dog, its breed, its date of birth and sex, the dog's registration number, the veterinarian's name, and the date of the X-ray. The film and a completed application form (by owner and veterinarian) are then mailed to the OFA for reading and diagnosis. The films should be placed in a stiffened, protective mailing envelope. If there are technical questions, the OFA may be reached at telephone number (314) 442-0418.

All results and diagnoses are kept confidential. Only the owner and the veterinarian are informed of the OFA's findings. If the hips are acceptable, the dog will be given a certification number that, for the Shar-Pei, will begin with the letters "SP." This number can then be used in all official identifications of the animal. Since clear hips are a highly desirable trait, many breeders will state in their advertising whether the animal has been OFA approved. Prospective buyers should request to see the official OFA certification papers if there is any question as to the dam and/or sire's hip status.

An approach similar to a European method is beginning to be available in the United States. It involves taking X-rays of the relative angles of the dog's femoral head and neck. By comparing those results against a set of "normal" standards, an estimate of the dog's future hip status can be made. However, the X-ray MUST be taken exactly at six months of age otherwise the results will be inaccurate. Essentially, the greater the angles' values, the greater the possibility of hip dysplasia at maturity. Over a certain degree, breeding of these animals is discouraged. As in most testing, grey zones do exist. In this case, it is suggested that the X-ray be repeated at one year of age, or waiting until the required two years of age by the OFA. In any case, this technique is usually only necessary when a young animal is being stringently evaluated for its potential breeding capabilities.

The impact of hip dysplasia on the conscientious breeder is obvious. The only means of eradicating this condition is by careful, selective breeding of certified, dysplasia-free animals. Since the condition is polygenic, even dogs that are overtly clear may be harboring the condition or the potential. The professional consensus is that the only actual way to eliminate the condition is by progeny testing. This is done by following successive litters of offspring of cleared parents over a period of time and determining, by testing the growing pups, whether or not the parents are in fact dysplasia-gene free. In a sense this is, genetically, looking backwards and forwards. For the breeder it entails much work and follow-through; however, the end result would mean a clear gene pool that would serve as the foundation for all future generations. What this also means, in reality, is that the current pool of breeding stock must be carefully and objectively reviewed. In the case of the Shar-Pei, where the total number of dogs is relatively small to begin with, the breeder must look to breed only the best-of-the-best. As the gene pool improves over time, breeders can become increasingly stringent in their requirements for sires and dams.

The Professional Services Division of Kal Kan offer breeders these tips for a dysplasia-reducing breeding program:

- Breed only normal dogs to normal dogs.
- The normal dogs should come from normal parents and grandparents.
- The normal dogs should come from litters in which greater than 75% of the siblings are normal.
- Choose a sire that has a record exceeding that of the breed average for producing normal progeny.
- Choose replacement bitches that have better hip joint conformation than that of their parents and that of the breed average.
- As the frequency of dysplasia is lowered, raise the standard for selecting "superior" sires and bitches.

The goal of treatment for dysplastic animals is relief of discomfort and return of as normal an activity level as possible. While the condition cannot be cured nor the degenerative process halted, the symptoms can be controlled.

Although the hip joint itself does not have any pain receptors, the surrounding joint capsule, ligaments and bone do. As the condition progresses, the malalignment places undue wear on these supportive tissues, leading to their inflammation, and resulting pain and stiffness. Pain is controlled at this first stage by the use of a buffered aspirin, such as Ascriptin or Bufferin. A dose of five grains per 25 pounds of body weight, or 25 mg per kilogram of body weight, every eight hours with food is used. Aspirin, while an effective pain reliever, is also a anticoagulant. As a result, the dog should be watched for the fortunately rare complication of abnormal bleeding: bruising of the skin or any unusual bleeding. These are signals that the dog is not tolerating the drug. A more common side effect of aspirin treatment is gastric upset, producing nausea, vomiting and anorexia. Any sign that the dog is experiencing difficulty with the drug should be immediately reported to the veterinarian.

As the disease progresses, aspirin may no longer control the discomfort. Another drug, Butazolidine, is used in severe cases of hip dysplasia. This drug has gained a poor reputation due to its misuse in the treatment of race horses, as it makes the animal feel so well that it overextends itself with disastrous results. With appropriate activity regulation, "Bute" is extremely successful in treating the discomfort of dysplasia. Although an effective drug, Bute has been known to cause blood changes in some animals and may require blood monitoring.

Some animals respond to a host of newer, non-steroidal agents, such as Motrin. This group of man-made drugs act as an anti-inflammatory, reducing pain and fever. They have proven very successful in treating long-term cases of hip dysplasia which could not be safely handled with true steroids. The side effect of this drug category is gastric and intestinal irritation. Giving the drug on a full stomach should lessen the impact.

In some cases steroidal anti-inflammatories may be given. Prednisone or Prednisolone are given at the rate of 0.5 to 1.0 mg per kilogram of body weight. (Divide the number of pounds by 2.2 to get number of kilograms) Careful monitoring of the animal is required due to the side effects of steroids.

Steroids and aspirin may be used simultaneously, but the total potential for serious side effects is also increased. Gastric bleeding is the most common difficulty and must be vigilantly watched.

Since many dogs that are requiring treatment are older, the possibility of underlying decreased kidney function is high. All of these drugs, aspirin, steroids or Bute, are filtered through the kidney in order to excrete them from the body. In the older dog with decreased kidney function, toxic levels of the drug could develop rapidly. It is reasonable to assume that all dogs of advanced years have some degree of limited filtering ability and must be monitored carefully.

In addition to drug treatment, physical therapy is of benefit to the dysplastic dog of any age. Walking or swimming are the best forms of activity. Any strenuous, exertive or prolonged activity should be prevented. Housing quarters should be warm and dry, with bedding soft and well padded. Weight control of the dysplastic animal is *IMPERATIVE*! Any excess load on the already damaged joint will only hasten the degenerative process and cause what might have been minor complications to intensify. The neutered animal with its tendency to acquire unneeded pounds must be carefully fed. Over-weight dogs may be dieted under the direction of the veterinarian.

In severe cases surgical intervention may be necessary. In lighter dogs a procedure called resectional arthroplasty can be done to modify the hip joint and reduce the pain. This method is typically used in small, lighter weight or older animals (which lead a more sedentary life style) where the joint is not exposed to tremendous force or stress. The femoral head is removed from the top of the long leg bone. This new "top" is then located between where the head of the femur originally was and the hip cup. Fibrous tissue forms around these two structures and holds the femur firmly in place to form a new joint. Obviously, a healthy leg and hip muscle mass are required for the success of the technique. This procedure takes away most of the pain and inflammation associated with the old joint. Many dogs, particularly the smaller sized, live fully active lives with this sort of artificial "joint." For Shar-Pei, however, the results with this surgery have not been encouraging. Since the Shar-Pei is a moderately sized dog, the added weight on the hip joint can cause a resectional arthroplasty to deteriorate over time.

A newer method gaining supporters around the country is the total replacement of the hip joint. Oddly, this method was developed for humans, using the dog as a test model, but was never routinely applied to the general dog population. Ohio State University and the University of Florida are leading the research on canine hip replacement. The two-hour surgical technique involves replacing the dog's joint with a five inch, stainless steel artificial ball joint. The method also replaces the acetabulum with a plastic cup that will correctly stabilize the steel "bone." This specialized surgery is not available everywhere. At present only a few veterinary hospitals can afford the staggeringly expensive equipment. The procedure must be done under extremely sterile conditions since the danger of post-operative infection is great. Dr. Parker at the University of Florida performs the surgery in a special operating room equipped with air filters to decrease airborne bacteria. It takes approximately four to six weeks to recover from the operation but the wait appears worth it. The success rate for Dr. Parker's team is an impressive 90%.

Some of the larger American research centers are joining with European and Canadian research centers in an attempt to share medical research data and findings. They are attempting to standardize all testing for dysplasia so that there would be a universally accepted rating system. This would certainly assist in the evaluation of dogs imported from other countries. This spirit of collaboration may herald a positive era for hip dysplasia, as centers would no longer have to duplicate research. International cooperation would be of benefit to all.

Although a difficult condition to eradicate, hip dysplasia has been successfully decreased by diligent breeding practices. In Germany, the Shaferhund Verein, their equivalent to the German Shepherd Dog Club of America, refuses animals for registration unless they possess radiographically healthy hips. As a result of this strict requirement, the Germans have made giant inroads in the removal of hip dysplasia from their Shepherd stock. It is hoped that with a professional, objective approach to the cause and treatment of hip dysplasia in the Shar-Pei, it will in the near future become a disease of the past.

PATELLA LUXATION

Next to hip dysplasia, patella luxation is one of the most common causes of canine rear-quarter orthopedic problems. Although considered an independent disorder, it is in actuality the result of multiple defective interactions between bones, ligaments and muscles. It is impossible to completely separate one bone or joint problem from another due to their synergistic action. The old song points out this interconnectedness:

the ankle bone is connected to the shin bone, the shin bone is connected to the knee bone, and so on. In man or animal, a defect in one area telescopes up or down the skeletal chain.

The massive quadricep muscle lies on the front aspect of the femur, or thighbone, narrowing in diameter so that at its arrival at the kneecap it has formed into a tough, strong tendon called the quadricep tendon. The patella, or knee-cap, is actually the lower extension of the quadricep tendon which stabilizes the tendon. This tendon attaches to the upper portion of the patella with a thin fiber layer continuing over it to become the patellar ligament. The patellar ligament then continues farther down the leg to attach to one of the dog's lower leg bones, the tibia.

In the normal stride of the dog, there are two extremes of position within a dog's range of motion: extension and flexion. As the leg is brought forward to take a step, the leg is carried into position in a knee-bent, or flexed, position. As the dog lowers his foot to the ground and applies force to push forward, the leg is progressively straightened. As he drives ahead, the leg, at the end of the stride, is in full extension. The limb is then flexed and brought forward as this process repeats itself. This system of extension and flexion serves to propel the dog and is the fundamental process of locomotion.

Although small in size, the patella is a major, although passive, component of the rear leg. During movement the quadricep muscles exert a pull that radiates down the various structures: the quads contract, the patella is moved slightly upward, the patella ligament applies traction to the tibia, and the leg is extended. The patella rides smoothly in a groove, the trochlear groove, which serves to keep the tiny bone in proper position. When the quads relax, the patella slides back down into its anatomical position, the traction on the tibia is re-leased, and the leg is returned to its relaxed position.

In the normal leg, the force of the muscular contraction is applied in an orderly manner so that each individual structure completes its function with the least amount of wear and tear. Thus, the force of the contraction is transmitted in perfect alignment to the various structures. Structural difficulties arise when the transmission of the muscular contraction does not relay evenly. If a structure is out of alignment or one or more components are misshapen, the effort exerted is "off center" and can create abnormal stresses on the joint. Animals with faulty alignment most frequently present with gait abnormalities, joint dislocations or arthritic changes.

Patellar luxation is one of the most common consequences of misaligned rear limbs. Common in small breeds such as the Poodle, Yorkshire Terrier, Chihuahuas, Pomeranians, and Pekingese, it is also seen in the Chow Chow and the Shar-Pei. Luxation of the patella may be either medial or lateral, in that it slips to either the "inside" or "out-

Lateral patellar luxation.

side" aspect of the knee joint. Of the two, the medial form is the most common.

A dog may develop medial or lateral patellar luxation by congenital predisposition or by trauma. Congenital disorders tend to involve both rear legs, while traumatic injuries usually involve only one. In addition, lateral luxation is frequently associated with a concurrent hip dysplasia. Thus, for the breeder, the congenital form of either variety is of concern.

In the Shar-Pei luxations of both the medial and lateral types are seen. Some lines of Shar-Pei seem to have a higher propensity for this condition as a whole. This disorder needs to be assessed by a veterinarian and the appropriate treatment recommended according to the degree of severity.

Dog displaying typical stance of patellar luxation.

In medial luxation the most typical patient is an overweight animal. The dog has difficulty completely extending his legs and may crouch when standing still. Often the dog will have an abnormal stride, although in milder cases he may be asymptomatic. A classic characteristic of the disorder is a "skipping" step: the animal is walking normally and then suddenly will skip or hop for one or more steps. His gait then returns to normal. In other cases, the animal may jump off an object and cry out. He may "kick" his affected leg backward and then appear fine. These strange behaviors are caused by the patella slipping up over the trochlear groove while the leg is in the extended position. In milder cases, the patella will return to its normal position as the limb is moved, however it can become fixed in the abnormal position. In this more severe case, the patella must be manually replaced into the trochlear groove. This replacement technique should be left to the veterinarian in order to prevent further trauma to the joint.

Lateral patellar luxation is more frequently seen in large dogs. These animals have difficulty extending the legs and will display a crouching, knock-kneed stance with toes pointing out from the body. As in medial luxation, the degree of severity will determine the required treatment.

Many factors can generate the tendency for patella luxation. Improper angulation between the femur and the patella, bowed legs, knock-knees, shallow trochlear groove, congenitally misshapen bone and joint tissue, or forward tipping of the stifle may be at the root of this condition. The earlier in the dog's life the condition appears, the more severe is the disorder and the more radical the necessary medical treatment. (Some animals may first show signs as early as three to seven months of age.) Furthermore, the longer the condition remains unresolved, the more accentuated will be the degenerative process.

Breeders should try to decrease the incidence of traumatic luxation by taking preventive measures: young pups should be given solid footing while malleable bones are developing; tile or vinyl flooring avoided; and jumping restricted

Patellar luxation.

until the animal has finished its developmental growth. Tie-out chains are hazardous due to their tendency to wrap around the knees, causing torsion of the lower leg.

In medium-sized dogs very minor injuries to the knee may be resolved by rest and anti-inflammatory drug treatment. However, for many cases surgical intervention is required. In the moderately severe cases, the joint muscle and ligament capsule is modified to prevent the patella from riding out of its groove, and any uneven muscular pull is corrected. In the most severe cases, surgical remodeling of the trochlear groove and tibia is necessary.

Should the animal have bilateral luxations, one approach is to surgically correct the most severe leg first. Once that leg has completely healed, the second leg is treated. There is evidence, however, that by doing one leg at a time, the dog may tend to favor the corrected leg and delay its return to full weight-bearing. For this reason, some practitioners will surgically correct both knees simultaneously. The dog must then use both legs evenly, forcing maintenance of muscle tone and shortening the overall healing time.

Post-operative care of the dog is conservative. The incisional site is bandaged. Care must be taken that the animal does not attempt to remove the bandage or sutures. An Elizabethan collar may be required. For approximately three weeks, activity is restricted to short leash walks for elimination purposes only. Stairs, slippery surfaces, and other hazards are to be avoided. In the obese dog, a controlled weight-loss program should be instigated under veterinarian supervision. Generally, the owner should adjust the food intake of even the normal weight dog since his activity level will be greatly reduced.

Patella luxation is one orthopedic

Puppy at six weeks beginning to show signs of carpal weakness.

disorder where the prognosis for the animal is excellent.

CARPAL LAXITY

Proper growth and development in the dog involves both large and small joints. Defects in the larger joints such as the hip logically cause major ramifications in the movement of the animal. Some joints, while small, also directly impact the quality of mobility in the canine. The carpal joint of the front legs is one such area.

The dog's front legs are composed of three major bones that successively interconnect: the humerus begins at the shoulder joint and eventually forms the elbow joint with the radius and ulna bones of the forearm. As these two bones continue downward they meet the seven carpal bones at the "wrist" joint. This wrist is surrounded by a fibrous supporting capsule and various ligaments. One, the palmar ligament, is the major supporting structure of the carpal joint. Below the wrist the metacarpals and phalanges create the dog's actual foot and toes.

The carpal joint in the dog plays an important role in the movement of the front limbs. As the dog steps ahead, the carpals flex and allow the leg to be lifted up from the ground and placed forward. During the lifting movement of the opposite front leg, the first leg bears the entire weight of the front half of the animal. Since the front legs normally bear 75% of the dog's entire body weight, the carpals must withstand a tremendous load during locomotion.

A most common disorder of the carpal joints is subluxation, or laxity. This disorder is characterized by weakening of the carpal joint's supporting tissues, especially the palmar ligament, with consequent bone alignment alterations. By approximately three months of age the puppy can begin to show signs of the disorder. The wrist joint's position, instead of being in line with the rest of the leg, begins to slowly settle downward toward the "back" of the foot. As the dog gains weight associated with his normal growth, the condition worsens

A pup displaying carpal laxity and splayed toes.

Carpal Laxity in the Shar-Pei. Courtesy of J.W. Alexander, D.V.M., Dean, Oklahoma State University's College of Veterinary Medicine.

as other joints hyperextend in an attempt to compensate for the faulty position.

Laxity is typically found in both front legs. As in many conditions, the degree of severity varies between individual animals. Typically, the earlier the condition appears, the more extensive is the joint involvement. In addition, one leg may be more severely affected than the other. For some, the condition is mild and does not interfere with normal movement, while in others the condition leaves the pup virtually crippled.

Certain research studies have proven that carpal laxity is a recessive, sex-linked genetic trait found in the large and giant breeds and, more recently, in the Shar-Pei. It was first recognized during a study of canine hemophilia blood disease. That research found that carpal laxity may be "carried" and passed along to the progeny. For this

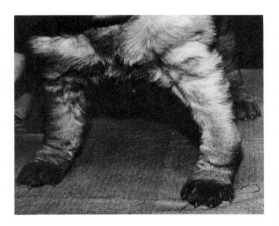

Carpal Laxity. Courtesy of J.W. Alexander, D.V.M., Dean, Oklahoma State University's College of Veterinary Medicine.

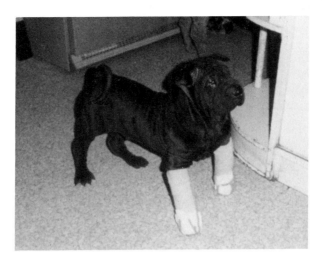

Example of foreleg splinting.

reason, affected animals are not appropriate candidates for breeding.

A study by Alexander and Earley found that, in examining twelve animals with the disorder, each had been environmentally influenced. Surprisingly, diet, with or without vitamin supplements, did not appear to have an impact on the development of the condition. The one common element among these affected young animals was that they were all raised on smooth surfaces or in small enclosures.

As a part of this study, the animals were treated by allowing unlimited exercise on grass or gravel. No changes were made in their diets. For severely affected pups, Mason metasplints were applied to give support to the legs. These supports remained on for two weeks while exercise was encouraged. If the carpal joint began to deteriorate after removal of the splint, it was reapplied. This exercise approach (with splint support for extreme cases) caused the majority of dogs to have major improvements in their joints within four to six weeks.

The conclusion was that in these genetically susceptible animals, the soft connective tissue of the carpal joint could not function properly without the proper strengthening associated with normal exercise. Similarly, smooth surfaces seem to place abnormal demands on the soft tissues, which are unable to mature fast enough to support the puppy's increasing body weight.

There are measures that can be taken to reduce the amount of stress on a developing carpal joint. Firm footing for the dog should always be provided in order to decrease the risk of trauma to the joints. Normal levels of exercise should be provided to promote normal bone, tendon, and muscle development. Jumping and other stressful activities should be discouraged, until at least six months of age, as susceptibility to stress fractures of the carpal joint is one frustrating complication of this condition. Since the weight of the patient is abnormally carried by the posterior surface of the carpus, any unusual trauma to the front legs may lead to fractures of the lower portion of the radius bone. It is not uncommon for untreated animals to suffer with repeated fractures.

Allowed to develop normally during the growth stage, these dogs can ultimately self-correct. However, any question of laxity of the wrist joint should be given prompt veterinary attention.

BOWED FORELEGS

Bowed forelegs is a condition that has received little direct research attention. As a result, the prevailing opinions about the disorder developed from what practitioners have experienced in the field. Dr. John McKibben, D.V.M. of Rome City, Indiana, recently reported this phenomena in a veterinary publication.

In the Shar-Pei, as many as one third of an affected litter could display bowed forelegs. Current data has not definitely pinpointed an hereditary link; however a strong familial tendency is suspected. The affected puppies will begin to display signs of the disorder by the fourth or fifth week of life. This condition is found almost exclusively in the front legs, although a few breeds do exhibit rear leg bowing. The Shar-Pei seem to confine this lateral bowing to the front legs, where carpal laxity may also be concurrently present. (See Carpal Laxity)

The exact cause of bowed forelegs is not yet known. It was once thought that the condition was related to the same factors that cause rickets in the human. In man, rickets is caused by a Vitamin D deficiency with associated calcium and phosphorus imbalances. This deficit does cause long-bone bowing; however, it also causes changes in the formation of the ends of the long bones. In the Shar-Pei condition, while the foreleg bones are bowed, the ends are not altered in shape or form. Since most practitioners now feel that these two disorders are not related, they merely refer to canine leg-bowing as "rickets-like."

Current research has proposed four basic areas that may initiate the structural problem: soft tissue immaturity, over-nutrition, environmental influences, and premature cessation of bone growth.

As in carpal laxity, one theory suggests the difficulty may arise from a mismatch between the rate of the animal's over-all growth and the ability of his soft tissues to support him. For some unexplained reason, the total growth of body mass and supporting structure are out of synchronization, causing excessive stress on the developing radius and ulna. The result could be an outward bowing. If this is in fact the case, these animals will be expected to "grow out" of the disorder as their skeletal structures and supportive soft tissues mature.

Similarly to carpal laxity, studies indicate that the environment of the animal may well influence its development. Slippery flooring, smooth surfaces and limited access to exercise may stress the supporting soft tissues and encourage improper growth of the long bones. These sort of external factors have been strongly tied to the development of carpal laxity.

Another theory is that the excessive stresses affecting the radius and ulna may be due to over-feeding with or without supplementation of vitamins and minerals. While these puppies may not be actually overweight, they are covertly carrying too much weight for their support tissues. One argument against this particular theory is that nutritional influences have been clearly ruled out as a cause of carpal laxity.

At the ends of the long bone are areas called the growth, or epiphyseal, plate. It is a thin layer of specialized cells that extends horizontally from one side of the bone to the other and serves as the focus from which new bone cells are added. As the cells increase in number, the bone gains length. These cells are added evenly and progressively so that the entire bone develops in a steady, uniform fashion. When the epiphyseal plates stop producing cells, growth is completed. All bones have their own specific internal clock and complete their growth accordingly. This process is usually completed in the Shar-Pei by 12 to 14 months of age.

The bowed leg condition resembles a primary premature closure of the growth plate disorder, but in the Shar-Pei the closure is believed to be secondary to the stress that the physical abnormality creates on the growth plate. Simply, the closure is triggered by the altered leg structure; the altered leg structure is not caused by a premature closure. Thus, it can be expected that as much as 25% of the bowed legs cases will have an eventual premature closure of at least one area of the growth plate in the leg bones.

It is believed that the tendency for premature closing of growth plates may be an inherited trait. Some lines within some breeds do seem to exhibit a greater susceptibility for this condition. Research has only been able to prove a recessive genetic association within the Skye Terrier breed. In relation to the tendency in the Shar-Pei, the data is not conclusive. Breeders may be wise to consider a genetic link should the condition repeatedly appear in their litters.

Factors that might elicit this premature plate closing are trauma, gross nutritional deficiencies, or chronically abnormal pressures such as obesity. Metabolic diseases affecting the parathyroid or kidney have also been implicated.

Whatever the initiating factor(s) of bowed forelegs, the consequences are elbow dysfunction and stress fractures of the leg and carpal bones. Affected animals are highly prone to joint dislocations due to their abnormal structural alignment. The unusual stress that this creates on the front legs will eventually lead to an accelerated deterioration of the front leg joints.

The prognosis for these animals is excellent since 78% straighten with time.

If the condition is severe, however, treatment is necessary to prevent the long-term ramifications of joint deterioration. The prevailing approach of treatment is to supplement the diet with additional calcium under a veterinarian's direction. In some cases, the legs may need to be placed in a cast until the soft tissues can support the body weight. Exercise should be consistent and moderate to encourage strengthening of the tissues. In addition, the dog should be sheltered from any hazardous activity or environment that might cause injury to the legs. Should the animal not respond to this conservative approach and the condition is potentially debilitating, surgical techniques are available. Ultimately, the comfort of the animal is the major concern.

JAW AND TEETH ABNORMALITIES

Whenever an animal is being considered for show or breeding, one of the first concerns is the mouth, specifically the jaw structure and bite. Their alignment can literally make or break the dog's show/breeding career. These two elements of jaw formation and teeth alignment cannot be separated, as one will ultimately influence the other. Even in the pet dog, with no lofty goals in mind, the correct oral conformation is important for adequate nutrition, health, and comfort of the animal.

The puppy begins its oral development

TOOTH DEVELOPMENT

	deciduous	permanent
incisors	3-4 weeks	2-5 months
canines	3 weeks	5-6 months
premolars	4-12 weeks	4-6 months
molars	none	5-7 months
total	**28**	**42**

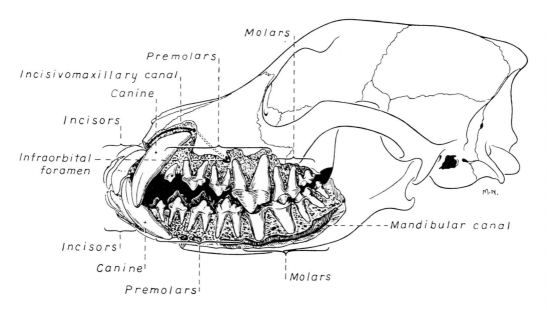

Molars
Premolars
Incisivomaxillary canal
Canine
Incisors
Infraorbital — foramen

M·N.

Mandibular canal

Incisors'
Canine'
Premolars'

Molars

Jaws and teeth of an adult dog. From Miller's Anatomy of the Dog. *Evans & Christensen, 1979.*

with the eruption of baby or deciduous teeth at around three to four weeks of life. Ultimately he will have a total of 28 deciduous teeth that include incisors, canines, and premolars. As the puppy grows, the deciduous teeth are gradually replaced with permanent teeth starting at around two to five months of age. The front teeth or incisors are the first to appear, followed by the premolars, the canines, and finally the molars.

During this replacement process, the roots of the baby teeth are absorbed as the adult tooth moves into the same location. In essence, the baby teeth are acting as guides for the position of the adult teeth. In some cases, the baby tooth does not fall out and the adult tooth is forced to "come in" alongside. This means that the adult tooth will be permanently out of proper alignment. In addition it can cause injury to the tissues of the mouth as well as abnormal tooth wear. For these reasons, puppies from three to six months of age should be checked monthly to be sure that no baby teeth are being abnormally re-

tained. Dental malalignment caused by retained deciduous teeth is one of the easiest to prevent! If a baby tooth is reluctant to come out on its own, it can be easily extracted by a veterinarian. By the time the dog is mature, he should have a total of 42 permanent teeth, although some dogs do have fewer. (In some Standards, less than the breed-specific number of teeth is a show-ring disqualification.)

The ultimate test of the dental development is the position of the jaw and teeth as they meet together in the bite. In most dogs, including the Shar-Pei, the expected bite should conform to a positional pattern called the scissors bite. This term refers to the top incisors slightly overlapping and touching the lower incisors. The premolars should then fit in an alternating pattern with the upper tooth coming between two lower teeth, very much like a jack-o-lantern's alternating toothy smile. These precise positionings create the best functional action with the least amount of wear.

Unfortunately, not all dogs are blessed with a perfect scissors bite. The relationship of the bite's position is actually one of the issues determining the quality of the dog, i.e. "pet" versus "show" quality. Some animals will have a bite that is just slightly "off" from a scissors bite called an even bite. In this pattern the incisors, instead of overlapping, meet end-to-end.

Some bite disorders include more dramatic deviations from the norm including overshot and undershot bites. When discussing the different bite formations, there is frequent confusion as to the exact meaning of these terms. For our purposes, the definitions used are those accepted by veterinarians: in referring to the relative position of the bite, it is the position of the *upper* jaw or maxilla which is the landmark. Therefore, in the overshot jaw, the top jaw and teeth protrude beyond the lower jaw and teeth. In the human this condition is commonly called "buck teeth," and in the dog it is called "parrot mouth."

Conversely, an undershot jaw refers to the top jaw and teeth being behind the lower jaw and teeth. This condition in some breeds such as the Bulldog and Boxer is considered normal; however, in most other breeds it is considered a fault. It frequently appears in the brachycephalic or brachycephalic-like breeds, such as the Chow Chow and Shar-Pei, where the facial structure of the head, and thereby the jaw, has been shortened. The difference between the length of the two jaws in both over- and undershot bites can be variable depending on the degree of abnormality.

A wry mouth refers to the two halves of the lower jaw growing at different rates so that one side is "longer" than the other. This is considered the most severe of jaw abnormalities.

It should be remembered, however, that the structure of the canine head and jaw continues to develop as the animal grows. Most breeds' jaws are not completely developed until the animal has reached its full maturity, which in the Shar-Pei is around one year. During that time the mandible grows at a more dramatic rate than the maxilla.

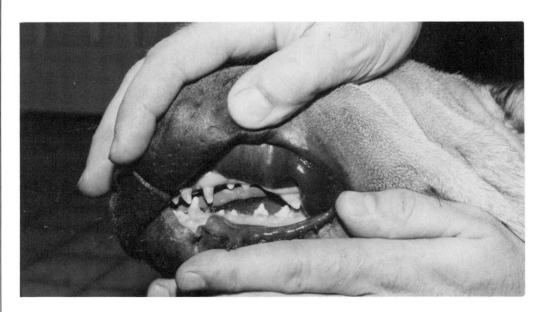

Abnormal dental arrangement of a five month old pup.

Overshot jaw	-Mendelian recessive
	-Modified recessive
	-Breeding between short-faced and normal muzzles
	-Recessive
Undershot jaw	-Breeding between short-faced and normal muzzles
Retained deciduous teeth	-Mendelian recessive

Therefore, a malalignment at an early age does not necessarily indicate that the mature animal will have the same defect. In fact, it is common to see that at say 20 weeks of age a perfect scissor bite can change to an undershot bite a few weeks later; an overshot bite at around 20 weeks of age can become a perfect scissors bite weeks later. Thus it is apparent the difficulty in predicting the final outcome of a particular bite.

No breed is exempt from deviations from the normal jaw configuration. The influence of heredity can be readily seen in the oral outcome. In some breeds such as the Dachshund, malocclusions have been proven to be a recessive trait, although this has not been conclusively proven in other breeds.

Faulty bites can be caused by the simple retention of baby teeth or by more complex conditions. Heredity, as evidenced by the over-all characteristics of the dog's jawbone, will dictate the resulting bite. The most complex causes of canine malocclusions are narrow lower jaws (mandibles), improper eruption and angulation of the canine teeth, and excess numbers of teeth. In the Shar-Pei, one other condition, a tight lower lip, can lead to malocclusion.

In some animals a narrowed structural characteristic of the jaw will create difficulties with the number and position of the teeth. The most obvious problem will be with the six lower incisors, which are easily shifted into abnormal positions. The jaw, as it tapers into the muzzle, becomes too narrow to accept the normal number of teeth. As a result, the teeth are forced into abnormal positions in order to fit. The treatment of choice is to remove the outer two incisors in order to allow the proper seating of the remaining four. Although this does not alter the underlying problem of the jaw's structure, it provides for proper eating and chewing action and less periodontal disease.

The position and angle of the canine teeth are also a common cause of malocclusion. When the mouth is closed in the normal dog, the upper canine tooth fits behind the lower canine tooth. If either of the canine teeth are improperly placed or their direction of angle is altered, the inter-meshing of this dental group will be off. Errant canine teeth can cause injuries to the soft tissue of the roof of the mouth and gums. If tooth hits tooth, the constant rubbing action can erode their enamel. Orthodontic measures should be taken.

In addition, the bite can be compromised by other features of the face and muzzle. In the Shar-Pei, some breeders prefer a full muzzle and mouth called a "meat-mouth" which gives the dog the characteristic "hippopotamus-look." While aesthetically appealing, it can generate a secondary condition called a tight lower lip that greatly hinders the proper positioning of the lower teeth and can compromise the dog's general health.

The tight lip disorder begins its destructive influence while the animal is young and the teeth in a malleable stage. The heavy lower lip tissue presses up and over the lower teeth, pushing the teeth inward from their normal position. Without intervention, the lip will fix the teeth in this abnormal position creating a permanent malalignment. The excess lip tissue can also interfere with proper eating since the dog bites the lip as he attempts to chew. Many of these animals have a secondary undernutrition due to the impinging lower lip.

It has been found that if the abnormal pressure of the lip can be removed early enough in the pup's dental development, the jaw's inherent ability to shift position may allow the animal's teeth to return to a normal bite. Many breeders begin to manually pull the lower lip forward and out, in a gentle stretching motion, as soon as the condition begins to appear. This approach takes dedication on the part of the owner as only repetitive stretching over a long period of time seems to have any permanent result.

Another method used to treat tight lip is tacking of the lower lip away from the lower teeth. Similar to eyelid tacking, it has unfortunately not had the same success; however, many owners prefer to begin with this approach. As with entropion, repeated procedures will need to be made. (See Entropion) The basic concept is that by keeping the lip away from the teeth until the dog is mature, the teeth stand a good chance of remaining in proper alignment.

Finally, surgical correction of the defect can be done. This procedure, also similar to entropion surgery, involves removal of an elliptical piece of tissue from the chin beneath the lower lip. In essence, the procedure is taking a "tuck" in the excess lip tissue. Some practitioners also include a second step whereby an incision is made in the inside of the lower lip, at the junction of the lip and the inner lower jaw. This incision is allowed to remain unsutured and serves to release some of the lip tension. Breeders have noted that within hours after the procedure the dog is comfortable and may eat as he has never done before!

This type of surgical technique must be done while the teeth and jaw are still developing. Most practitioners rec-

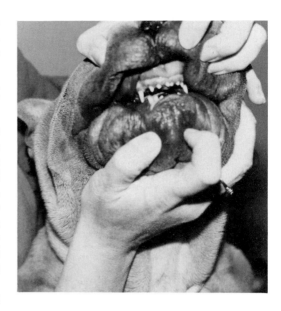

Example of tight lower lip. Without surgery, the bite would be altered due to the pressure of the lip on the lower teeth.

ommend doing the procedure at four to six months of age. Although older dogs having the correction will still benefit from the improved eating habits, the bite may never return to a totally normal scissors position.

Whenever dental malalignments exist, early correction is the best policy. In the past few years, veterinarian-dentists have begun to incorporate some of the same techniques used in humans. Dr. Randi Brannan, D.V.M. of Ohio is using extractions, acrylic plates and bridges, incline planes, palate expanders, and various wiring methods to change what was once usually a live-with-what-you-have situation. In most cases these methods are used for the comfort and health of the animal and not just for cosmetic affect. As with any type of corrective surgery, controversy has arisen over the use of orthodontic measures in show dogs, as the underlying structural, and possible genetic, defect still exists.

Although the future is promising for

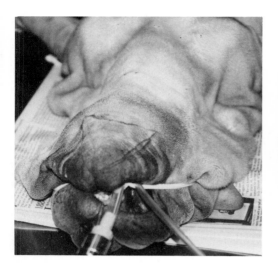

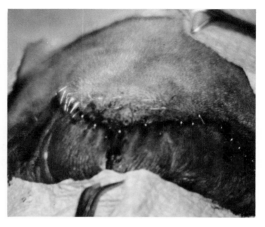

Placement of sutures in repair of tight lip.

Dog prepared for tight lip surgery. General anesthesia is used. The area of skin to be removed is carefully marked.

veterinary dentistry, the ultimate cure for all types of malocclusion lies in con-

scientious breeding for the correction. Over time, as in other orthopedic conditions such as hip dysplasia, the disorder can be eliminated from the breed by this method.

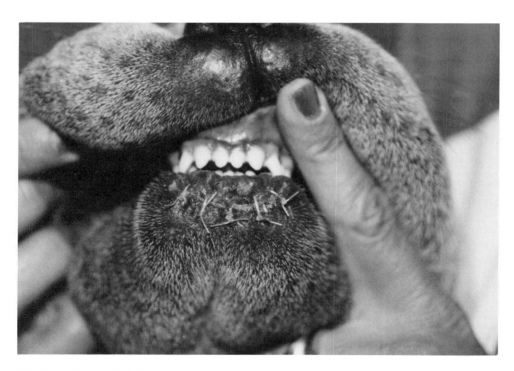

Healing phase of tight lip surgery.

A charming Yao'Shu's Cloisonne X Da Hei Xiong puppy. Margery Denton, photo.

A puppy in robust health. Yao'Shu's Cloisonne X Da Hei Xiong puppy. Margery Denton, photo.

CHAPTER SIX

EAR, NOSE AND THROAT DISORDERS

CANINE EAR PROBLEMS: CANAL STENOSIS AND OTITIS EXTERNA

A dog's hearing is one of his most developed senses. He relies on its acuity for orientation, defense and daily living. Conditions that interfere with the quality or transmission of sound jeopardize the dog's well-being. By far the most common ear diseases are confined to the outer ear and pinna. If untreated, they may progress into the deeper structures, thus causing permanent damage.

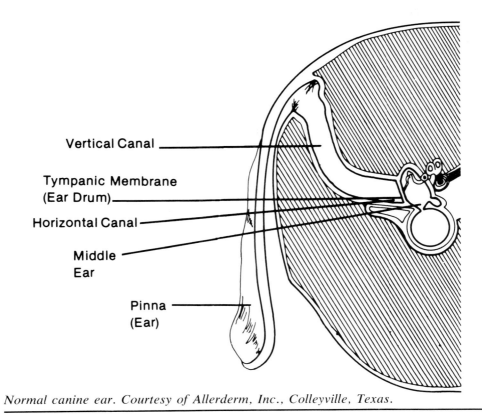

Vertical Canal

Tympanic Membrane
(Ear Drum)

Horizontal Canal

Middle
Ear

Pinna
(Ear)

Normal canine ear. Courtesy of Allerderm, Inc., Colleyville, Texas.

The canine ear is composed of four basic regions: the outer ear flap, or pinna, the ear canal, the middle ear structures and the inner ear structures. Each region has its own specialized function within the complex process of what we know as "hearing." Conditions in one region frequently impact the other regions, making treatment of even minor disorders imperative.

The process of hearing actually begins with the collection and relay of sound waves by the pinna. The shape of the ear is related solely to the specific breed and does not necessarily correspond to the acuteness of that breed's hearing. Whether the ear is long and hanging, small and close fitting, or erect and open, it serves as a channel for sound waves down the ear canal to the tympanic membrane, or ear drum. The movement and angulation of the ear itself is con-trolled by 19 muscles and numerous facial nerves. By adjusting the position of the ear, the dog is able to better "focus" the source and quality of the incoming sound.

In the Shar-Pei the ideal ear set is small and close fitting to the head. The standard calls for "thick, equilateral triangles in shape, slightly rounded at the tips. . . . Ears lie flat against the head, are set wide apart and forward on the skull, pointing toward the eyes." Whereas shape or position does not directly affect the quality of hearing, these physical characteristics may set the stage for recurring ear problems. Just as the Cocker Spaniel has a tendency toward ear infections due to the lack of air flow under the pendulous pinna, so the closely fitting position of the Shar-Pei's ear lends itself to poor air circulation.

The external ear canal descends downward at an almost 45 degree vertical angle for approximately half of the canal and then bends into a horizontal position for the remainder of the distance to the eardrum. The Shar-Pei's ear canal is much more narrow than the average 4 to 5 mm in the general dog population. This narrowness can, and often does, lead to problems with a build-up of cerumen (ear wax) due to its inability to escape during vigorous head-shaking.

The ear drum separates the external ear from its middle chambers' components. It is a thin, flexible flap of tissue that vibrates as sound waves bounce against it. On the inner side of the ear drum is the middle ear, composed of three small bones that interact in a precise manner. The slightest movement of the ear drum causes the bones to relay the movement to the inner ear chamber. In addition, cranial nerves present in the middle chamber send information about equilibrium to the brain.

The inner ear is responsible for accepting the transmission of the sound-generated movements of the tiny ear bones and altering it into a nerve impulse. The impulse is then sent to the brain, where its information is decoded and "recognized" by the animal. The inner ear is also equipped with structures, called semicircular canals, that do not pertain to hearing but to balance and spatial orientation. As a result, disorders of the middle and inner ear are serious in nature, as the structures are extremely delicate; inflammations can result in the animal's not being able to hear, stand or walk. This consequence, however, is fortunately rare if treatment is prompt.

The skin lining the external canal and pinna is composed of epithelial cells, sebaceous and modified apocrine glands. The aprocrine glands produce the cerumen that serves to coat and moisturize the outer ear structures. In the normal ear bacteria and yeast such as *Staph-ylococcus, Streptococcus* and *Malassezia,* are present but are kept in check. If the amount of cerumen increases, the diameter of the ear canal is further diminished and the consequent decreased air circulation, increased moisture, and dark, warm environment can set the stage for the over-proliferation of these organisms, often resulting in a disorder called otitis externa.

One of the most common ear conditions, otitis externa is seen in as many as 20% of the general dog population. In actuality otitis externa is a descriptive term for the disorder and its location. As the name indicates, the outer portion of the ear from pinna inward to the ear drum can be involved.

Pain is a common characteristic of otitis. The dog's desperate attempts to stop the pain often result in severe self-inflicted injury to the pinna. It is not uncommon for a hematoma, or large blood blister, to form as the pet scratches the painful ear. This sort of insult to the pinna is a serious problem in its own right and may cause permanent ear flap deformities. Thus, any ear disorder deserves prompt veterinary attention.

Otitis externa may be either acute or chronic in nature. Acute otitis is often caused by the presence of an object within the ear canal. With the presence of a foreign object, such as a tick or foxtail awn, the animal will suddenly display severe symptoms, usually only in one ear. In most cases the object will need to be retrieved by use of a long-nosed forcep or flushed out with a bulb syringe and solution. It is imperative that the animal be still during the procedure due to the potential for injury to the ear drum. If a foreign object is discovered, the accepted practice is to instill 10 to 15 drops of a topical anesthetic into the ear canal. By anesthetizing the ear canal, removal of any future items will also be facilitated as the animal will not be head-shy due to the negative experience. Should the dog still not be able to tolerate its removal, general anesthesia is necessary. Brute physical restraint of any dog during removal of an object is strongly discouraged.

Chronic otitis is usually a more gradual, bilateral condition that slowly intensifies over time. The owner is rarely aware of the problem until the condition is exaggerated. Typical causes of chronic otitis externa include a resistant organism, presence of mites, a tumor, an untreated acute condition or a part of a more involved medical complex. Habits of the pet such as swimming, bathing or other pets licking the ear can ignite a chronic response.

In chronic otitis conditions, the prolonged irritation and inflammation of the tissue lining the ear canal cause the secretory glands to enlarge and produce increased amounts of cerumen. Cerumen alters the skin's fatty acids, thereby chemically irritating the canal. It also provides a fertile ground for bacterial growth by encouraging increased humidity. The ear tissue responds to the irritation, humidity and resulting bacterial presence by swelling, inflammation and maceration. Otitis' odorous discharge is due to the infection and cerumen, each contributing a distinctive smell.

The Shar-Pei is particularly predisposed to chronic otitis due to the presence of cerumen, tight-fitting ear flaps and narrow ear canals. In an already narrow canal only a minor increase in the production of cerumen can produce the conditions of reduced airflow which favors the emergence of chronic otitis. Furthermore, the Breed Standards emphasize a close fitting ear flap that, while conformationally correct, can further aggravate a condition.

These infections are usually caused by the over-growth of *Staphyloccus, Streptococcus, Pseudomonas, Proteus* or yeast organisms. In many cases, more than one organism can be cultured from the same ear. Bacterial otitis is characterized by reddened, painful ears oozing an exudate, its properties corresponding to the type of bacteria present. A light yellow discharge is indicative of a gram-negative bacterial infection, while a tan discharge indicates a gram-positive infection.

Yeast infections are becoming more commonly recognized. Whenever excessive cerumen is present, or the normal PH of the ear canal is increased, yeasts are apt to over-multiply. One yeast, *Malassezia,* produces a moist, dark, almost black, discharge with a sweet odor.

Ear mites can produce chronic otitis externa. The condition is highly contagious and may be acquired from casual contact with other animals. The mites live and feed on the debris of the ear flap and canal. Their presence is highly irritating, causing ear twitching, scratching, rubbing and a thick, dry, brown or black "coffee-ground" discharge. While the entire life cycle of the mite is only three weeks, the ongoing process sets the stage for secondary bacterial infection in the inflamed ear tissue. Treatment of the affected animal is necessary as well as any other dogs or cats that live in the same environment.

Other conditions that produce and/or predispose to chronic otitis are seborrhea, allergies and hypothyroidism. One of the first symptoms that the owner notices may be ear inflammation. However, the ear inflammation is secondary to the underlying medical situation and cure revolves around correction of the primary disease entity. (See Seborrhea; Allergies; Hypothyroidism)

Tumors, while very uncommon, are much more gradual in their occurrence and are typically unilateral. In most cases, their presence is undetected until the condition is advanced. The prognosis for these animals is poor due to the difficulty in removing extensive tumors.

One consequence of a progressive, untreated ear infection is the rupture of the ear drum. It is important to treat this condition adequately since bacteria now have access to the middle and inner ear chambers. Left untreated, meningitis can develop. For this reason, more extensive ear flushing is necessary in order to remove the debris and organisms from the external and middle ear chambers. This procedure is done while the dog is under general anesthesia. Owners should be aware that the dog may sneeze or cough for a few days after treatment. Some animals will even cough when medication is applied into the ears, due to small amounts draining into the throat through the ruptured drum and middle ear chamber.

Visualization, diagnosis and treatment of otitis externa are dependent on a cerumen-clear pinna and ear canal. Therefore, if there is discharge present in the canal, initial cleansing of the ear serves the dual purpose of allowing a clear view for the veterinarian to make the diagnosis and preparing the otitic ear for treatment. Most ear antibiotic medications are inactivated in the presence of pus, making a clean ear imperative. In many cases cleansing can be done with a cooperative patient; however, general anesthesia may be necessary if the ear is extremely painful.

The ear discharge can then be examined by staining with Diff-Quik to ascertain whether a bacterial, fungal or yeast infection is present. Any black crusts should be examined for mite infestation. More extensive bacterial cultures can be performed if indicated.

Flushing of the ear with a cleansing agent is the most effective method of ear cleaning. There are many products on the market for this use such as Panoprep, Oticlens, Cerumenex, and Oticlean. Some practitioners even use a diluted solution of Betadine or Nolvasan. The ear canals are then carefully cleaned and dried by use of a bulb syringe or drying agent.

The ear canal is observed for physical signs of the condition. Frequently the canal will have ulcerations and macerations of the epithelial lining that will require medical treatment. If the canal is extremely swollen, anti-inflammatory drugs may be required before the vet can adequately inspect the canal.

Treatment of both acute and chronic otitis involves the frequent application of topical antibiotic ointments into the ear(s). The exact antibiotic used depends on the causative organism(s). In most cases, the drug companies combine multiple antibiotics in order to treat a wider range of conditions. In general, chloramphenicol, neomycin or gentamicin is used to treat bacterial infections; thiabendazole is used to treat mites; while miconazole, nystatin or clotrimazole is used to treat both yeast and fungal infections.

Most otitic antibiotic medications are packaged by the manufacturer with a plastic snout for reaching down into the ear canal. Care must be taken to prevent the snout from injuring the fragile, inflamed canal tissue. For many animals the application of ear ointment or solution may be a two-person ordeal!

In general, topical ear medications are liberally instilled into the vertical canal and the lower "bell" massaged so that, with gravity, the medicine will coat the entire tract. Once the medication is in the ear, most dogs enjoy the ear rubbing, leaning into the hand. When the massage is completed, the dog will classically shake its head, serving to spread the medicine onto the pinna and outer ear structures. Solutions are easier for the owner to apply since they move down the ear canal more readily; however, their "thinness" reduces their longevity in the ear. Ointments, on the other hand, are harder to instill properly, needing longer massage to spread adequately; however, they will remain in contact with the ear tissue longer.

Even with adequate antibiotic treatment, chronic cases of otitis may recur in two to six months. If infections are reappearing, environmental or allergic factors may be involved. Allergy tests may be indicated. In addition, the activities of the dog should be investigated: frequent swimmers often get repeated infections due to water entering the ear canal, hunting dogs are in frequent contact with plant spores, and dogs active in sandy soil may introduce grains into the tract. More extensive bacterial cultures should be performed to rule out a resistant strain of organism.

In some recalcitrant cases, a short-term treatment with steroids may be used to decrease aprocrine gland secretion and thereby decrease the production of cerumen. Similarly, the administration of a synthetic form of Vitamin A, has been found to decrease the glands' activity. While not a direct treatment of inflammation or infection, steroids and Vitamin A can alter the amount of cerumen, a major causative factor of otitis.

When it is determined that ear mites are the instigating factor, Tresaderm is the drug of choice. Three to five drops of solution are instilled into the ear canal twice daily for seven days. Some practitioners use a treatment schedule whereby the drops are instilled for ten days, stopped for ten days, and reapplied for ten days for a total of 30 days. This approach covers the entire mite life cycle from egg to maturation. Furthermore, many vets strongly recommend refrigeration of the drug to maintain its effectiveness. Some animals do experience a sensitivity to Tresaderm, so any increased redness, irritation or obvious distress should be reported to the practitioner immediately. Application to frank ulcerations is not recommended.

If otitis becomes unresponsive to medical intervention, surgery may be required. A procedure called a lateral ear canal resection is the method most commonly used. This technique removes the exterior wall of the vertical canal to increase air flow and reduce humidity and warmth; it also helps liquefied cerumen to exit the canal. While healing, the ear flap is placed up onto the top of the head. In the case of the Shar-Pei, their small ear flaps may have to be anchored in place with bandage tape. Some practitioners prefer to leave the surgical site open to air while others place a protective, absorbent bandage over the wound. (Many animals object to the feeling of a bandage and will head-shake or paw at the site. In that event, an Elizabethan collar should be used.) Dogs are treated with a systemic antibiotic for approximately two weeks. In general, healing takes 10 to 14 days; however healing, particularly in the older dog, may be lengthy. If the otitis fails to improve, a more radical surgical procedure to remove the entire ear canal may be the last resort.

Once the existing infection is controlled, at-home preventative measures can begin. Habits that encourage increased moisture should be avoided: pets should be discouraged from ear licking; and cotton should be placed into the ear canal prior to bathing. An ear drying agent such as Domeboro otic solution (3-5 drops per ear) will assist in the required thorough drying needed after bathing or swimming.

In some cases, appropriate owner care can also help to prevent wax build-up which encourages infection. Limited cleaning may be accomplished by judicious use of a Q-tip gently inserted into the ear canal to remove as much of the debris and discharge as possible. Great care must be taken to prevent the swab from pushing the exudate even farther down into the canal. In many cases, this procedure serves only to pile the debris against the ear drum and complicate further treatment. For this reason, swab-cleaning of the vertical canal by the owner should be done only after instruction from the veterinarian! Particularly in some Shar-Pei with very narrow ear canals, owner or groomer use of Q-tips may not be recommended.

Many vets recommend use of a ceruminolytic (wax solvent) agent such as Sebumsol once or twice weekly as a preventive measure. As with antibiotics, a liberal amount is placed into the ear canal. The lower portion of the ear, at its junction with the cheek, is gently massaged. After a few minutes the dog is then allowed to vigorously shake, which forces out the fluid. This procedure should obviously be conducted out of doors or in a washable environment! Once- or twice-weekly treatments are recommended in animals with recurring problems.

In addition, if the dog's ears are particularly close fitting, taping them up onto the head may help to increase air flow. Some practitioners recommend that they remain in the elevated position for seven to ten days whenever irritation is present. Johnson and Johnson makes a porous, breathable cloth tape called Zonas that is used by athletes during competition. It is very sticky yet easy to remove. Available in one- and two-inch widths, it is particularly useful in ear taping. However, whenever taping an ear, care should be taken to tape lightly. The ear should be checked three or four times a day to be certain that the blood supply to the tips is adequate. Any swelling, pain or discoloration would indicate that the ear has been taped down too tightly and the bandage should be removed and a vet consulted.

Attention to the status of the ears should be a part of the Shar-Pei owner's daily inspection of his pet. The saying "an ounce of prevention is worth a pound of cure" is definitely applicable to the Shar-Pei ear. Fortunately, disorders of the external ear fully respond to medical treatment. The quality of home treatment in most cases will be the deciding factor as to its effectiveness. Rigid adherence to the medical regime, although problematic for many owners with uncooperative pets, is essential.

BRACHYCEPHALIC AIRWAY SYNDROME

Breeds such as the Bulldog, Boxer, Boston Terrier, Pug, Pekingese, and Shih Tzu, where the face and muzzle profile is characteristically "flattened," share a common legacy of respiratory disorders. Caused by the inherent distortion of the upper airways, these disorders are also found in lesser degrees in the Shar-Pei and Chow Chow. The resulting respiratory problems, sometimes severe enough to constitute a medical emergency, are typically caused by the concurrent presence of narrowed nostrils (stenotic nares), elongated soft palate and the secondary changes to the larynx which these unusual head structures create. This complex of physical conditions is known as the brachycephalic airway syndrome.

The normal canine muzzle is divided roughly in half, horizontally from the nose back into the throat by a bony structure called the hard palate. This hard palate serves as the floor of the nose and the ceiling of the mouth. Unless there is a structural defect, known as a cleft palate, the two areas are totally separated. At the rear of the dog's mouth, the hard, bony palate turns into a soft tissue structure, called the soft palate, which projects part way into the animal's upper throat. The nose, in turn, beginning at the nostrils, or nares, continues backward in two separate channels until they merge into the rear of the mouth at the terminal end of the soft palate. This common meeting area is called the pharynx.

The pharynx is actually a "crossroads" where the mouth and nose structures end and the throat structures begin. From this point onward the throat divides into two tubes which serve completely different functions: the trachea, or windpipe, connects the nose to the lungs; the esophagus, or foodtube, connects the mouth to the stomach.

In the normal dog, these two tubes share the pharynx yet are able to keep their functions coordinated and separate. Food is channeled into the esophagus while swallowing and air is directed down the trachea. The coordination of these actions, swallowing and breathing, is dependent on a small structure called the epiglottis. The superior aspect of the tracheal tube is actually a specialized unit called the larynx, or voice box. The epiglottis is attached to the lower part of the front of the larynx. As the dog begins to swallow, the epiglottis moves backward to cover the entrance to the larynx and lower tracheal tube. Once swallowing is completed, the epiglottis moves forward to allow unobstructed breathing. In this fashion, food is usually prevented from "going down the wrong tube," or entering the larynx and trachea. Simply, the epiglottis functions as a "lid" for the lower respiratory system.

In the conventional canine muzzle, the soft palate does not overlap when the epiglottis is in the open position. In breeds where the muzzle is shortened, however, the length of the soft palate and the position of the epiglottis is the same as in a conventional muzzle, whereas the amount of room between the two may be radically decreased. It is the distance between these two structures that is altered by breeding for a structural change in the face or head, not the relative size of the internal structures themselves. What results is an exaggerated overlap of the soft palate tissue onto the epiglottis. In this position, the soft palate is subjected to irritation.

Changes in the skull formation may also telescope into other respiratory organs, causing varying degrees of physical distortions. The most frequent consequence is a narrowing of the nostrils, or stenosis of the nares. Common in the Shar-Pei, noisy breathing and difficult inhalation, particularly under stress, are the primary overt symptoms. Stenotic nares are very frequently found in association with changes in the soft palate, these defects being the principal characteristics of Brachycephalic Airway Syndrome.

The narrow nostrils predispose these dogs to abnormal breathing patterns. As the dog struggles to obtain oxygen, he must exert tremendous effort to inhale. The force required may be so great that the tissue of the soft palate becomes inflamed which in time leads to thickening and further elongation. The larynx also has areas which are subjected to damage from the inspiratory effort. Small out-pouchings of the laryngeal tissue are drawn into the throat's lumen and become inflamed and the supporting cartilage of the trachea will weaken. The distortion and encroachment of these tissues into the airway further impedes respiration, creating a potentially ominous condition.

Most animals, due to the altered head structure, will display symptoms from birth. Owners will notice frequent snorting, noisy breathing or snoring at night. If excited, the animal, especially puppies, will open-mouth breathe. Unable to tolerate the demands of exercise, these animals are quickly "winded." Some animals are able to lead fairly normal lives; however, these affected animals, if subjected to strenuous activity, high environmental temperatures, emotional stress or physical illness are highly susceptible to sudden distress called respiratory distress syndrome. Acute respiratory distress is characterized by severe breathing difficulty on the inhale and/or the exhale breath with cyanosis of the gums and inside lining

RESPIRATION

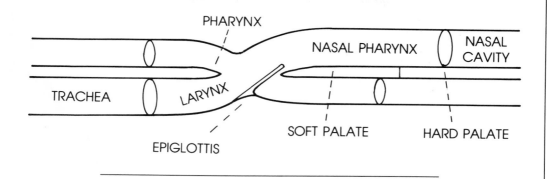

SWALLOWING

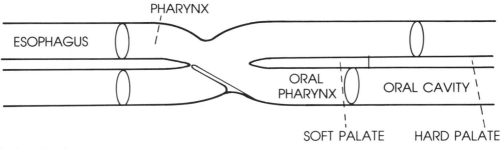

Canine Trachea and Esophagus.

of the eyelids. (Use of the eyelids is recommended as it may be difficult to assess the typical Shar-Pei with their darkly pigmented tongue and oral mucous membranes.) The animal may totally collapse. This is a medical emergency that must receive veterinary treatment IMMEDIATELY!!

Treatment of acute crises calls for immediate action to provide an open airway. The vet may need to create one by making an incision directly into the throat, called a tracheostomy. Oxygen is then provided. Later, as the causative structural abnormalities can be addressed, the tracheostomy may be closed.

Diagnosis for chronic conditions depends on the presence of clinical signs and examination of the throat's interior with a laryngoscope. In older animals when the disorder has been present for a period of time, X-rays may be necessary to determine the degree of internal changes. Most practitioners attempt to schedule the examination and the surgical treatment for the same time since the animal would then need to be anesthetized only once.

Treatment of chronic cases usually involves a three-step approach. The first step is to decrease the load on the dog's respiratory system by providing oxygen, cage rest, and cool environmental temperatures. The second step is to decrease any present edema in the various throat tissues by giving steroid medication. And finally, any obstructing elements within the airway must be surgically corrected. This technique involves a widening of the nostrils, excision of any interfering soft palate, and removal of any impeding laryngeal tissue. Most practitioners believe that the simultaneous correction of all contributing factors is necessary in order to provide the maximum effect with a minimum amount of stress.

Since stenotic nares is considered the primary cause of this syndrome, correction of at least that portion of the problem is recommended as early as possible. For severely affected puppies, the surgery may be done as early as three to four months of age. Studies show that correction at a young age has a major impact in terms of the prevention of more severe future consequences. Apparently, when an animal can breathe normally through its nose, the throat tissue is less traumatized and therefore less apt to begin the chronic cycle of swelling and obstruction.

Breeding for head form without concern for the relative proportions of the internal structures is the basic cause of this condition. Therefore, breeding for less exaggerated head structures is the only true "cure" for brachycephalic airway syndrome. For this reason, any animal that has required veterinary treatment for this type of respiratory abnormality should not be used for breeding. Just as in the treatment of other orthopedic conditions, the ultimate eradication of the disorder from the breed depends on conscientious breeding of non-affected animals to non-affected animals. Furthermore, it is possible to maintain the desired characteristic facial features while still using careful, selective breeding. Highly exaggerated head formations, because of their underlying physical handicaps, should be strongly discouraged.

MEGAESOPHAGUS

In the normal dog the esophagus begins just behind the rear of the mouth in the region called the pharynx. (See Brachycephalic Airway Syndrome) From there it descends downward within what is normally considered the "throat." At the beginning of the dog's "chest," the esophagus continues in an almost horizontal position and in close proximity to the lungs and heart. At the bottom of the esophagus is a sphincter, called the cardiac or lower esophageal sphincter, which prevents the reflux of stomach contents. Unlike man, who is able to use gravity to help deliver food from the mouth to the stomach, the dog propels its food by wave-like motions of the walls of the esophagus, called peristalsis.

The term megaesophagus refers to a dilatation of a portion of the esophagus. This dilatation usually occurs just above a structural defect. The defect can be a stricture, an abnormality of the muscles or nerves to that region, a defect in the lower esophagus sphincter, or an injury to the tissues due to trauma or surgery. In addition, some disease conditions such as Addison's, hypothyroidism, and lead poisoning can lead to the same symptoms. (See Hypothyroidism; Addison's Disease)

Megaesophagus is found in many breeds including the Shar-Pei. The German Shepherd, Great Dane and Newfoundland are suspected of having a familial tendency to megaesophagus, while a direct hereditary link has been found in the Wire-hair Fox Terrier and the Miniature Schnauzer. The disorder appears to affect males and females equally. Since there is the possibility of transmitting this condition to offspring, breeders are cautioned against breeding affected animals, or animals that have previously produced affected progeny.

Two forms of megaesophagus are recognized: acquired and congenital. Once grouped together under the same name, two distinctions are now made: acquired achalasia (AA) and congenital idiopathic megaesophagus (IME). The basic distinction between acquired and congenital rests on the age of onset of the disorder: acquired generally appearing in the mature animal and congenital appearing in the young dog. If an affected animal has ever had a history of problems as a young dog, the disorder is considered congenital; if a mature animal with signs has never had a history of problems as a young dog, the condition is considered acquired.

Acquired megaesophagus can be caused by many factors. Esophageal strictures from lesions, tumors, foreign bodies and surgical scar tissue can ultimately result in the accumulation of food and the resulting esophageal dilatation. Diseases of the nerves and/or muscles to that portion of the throat may be the root of the problem. Malignancies impinging on the esophagus can reduce the size of the lumen and alter food movement, creating an accommodating dilatation.

Congenital megaesophagus can involve defects in the structure of the esophagus and surrounding tissues. One common defect is in the coordination of the esophagus and the lower esophageal sphincter. In most cases food is carried to the stomach by peristalsis. As the food approaches the stomach, the lower esophageal sphincter opens to allow the food to enter. Once past, the sphincter closes to prevent food and stomach acids from refluxing back up into the esophagus. In affected animals, however, there may be a defect in the interaction of swallowing and the opening of the sphincter. For some reason, the sphincter delays in opening and food accumulates in the area just above it. Whatever the causative factor(s) for this lack of coordination, over time the esophagus dilates to accommodate the food bolus.

Another cause of megaesophagus is the persistence of an embryonic heart vessel that encircles the esophagus. In normal development, this errant vessel is usually replaced as the heart and surrounding structures mature. For an unknown reason, in some animals the vessel remains and constricts the esophagus, causing dilation. Finally, some cases are classified as idiopathic as no exact causative factor can be identified. This idiopathic variety is the

---

MAJOR CAUSES OF MEGAESOPHAGUS

Idiopathic factors
Esophageal Strictures
Vascular Developmental Anomalies
Neuromuscular Diseases:
   Myasthenia Gravis
   Polymyositis
   Systemic Lupus Erythematosus
Metastic neoplasms
Trauma
Surgery

---

most common form found in the Shar-Pei and is the area of present research.

The symptoms of both AA and IME are similar. Chronic regurgitation is the major sign. In congenital megaesophagus, a puppy begins to show signs at the time of weaning. Frequently these pups start to eat and then abruptly leave the dish. It is believed that the increased substance of the provided food, unlike mother's milk, has difficulty passing down the abnormal esophagus. Regurgitation occurs most frequently one to two hours after eating. The food is obviously undigested. As a result, vital nutrition is lost and leaves the animal thin, with poor coat and tissue quality. Coughing, difficulty breathing and in-

BREEDS SUBJECT TO MEGAESOPHAGUS

German Shepherd
Doberman Pinscher
Great Dane
Labrador
Irish Setter
Dachshund
Pomeranian
Chow Chow
Schnauzer
Golden Retriever
English Setter
Cairn Terrier
Brittany Spaniel
Wire-haired Terrier
Cocker Spaniel
Shetland Sheepdog
Irish Wolfhound
Poodle
Pug
Shar-Pei
Boxer

creased drooling can be present. Bulging of the throat can be seen in some cases. Inhalation pneumonia, caused by the "breathing-in" of fluid or food particles, is a major complication of megaesophagus.

Diagnosis of the condition is made by radiographs and fluoroscopy using swallowed barium to assess the motility of the esophagus. Laboratory tests to rule out hypothyroidism or Addison's disease should be conducted.

Female puppy with megaesophagus.

The most elemental principle in the care of these dogs is the prevention of inhalation pneumonia. Dogs with megaesophagus are overwhelmingly prone to inhalation pneumonia, a condition which carries an alarming 70% mortality rate. Enormous care is required on the part of the owner in order to prevent its occurrence. Thus, the basic regime is focused on the control of regurgitation and the aggressive treatment of pneumonia.

At the first sign of respiratory complications a bacterial culture of the esophagus should be taken. It is IMPERATIVE that the proper antibiotic be used to treat a threatening pneumonia. Without cultures, a particular antibiotic may be chosen that does not effectively battle the offending organism. By the time it is apparent that the drug is not working, it may be too late to save the animal.

The dog's food should be thinned into a watery/liquefied gruel. This consistency will help the bolus to pass. Smaller portions should be fed two to three times a day with the dog in an upright position, standing on his rear legs. For larger, mature animals, the food can be placed on a table in order to force the dog to stretch upward to reach the bowl. Once eating is completed, the dog should remain in the elevated/rear-standing position for at least ten minutes. Small puppies can be held in position on the lap for that time span; larger dogs can be placed on a staircase with the head and forelegs on an upper stair and the rear quarters on the floor. On *no* occasion should the animal be left alone while in this position, as it can not be guaranteed that he will remain in the prescribed angle.

One study indicates that a third of the congenital cases "grow out" of the problem, if death by pneumonia can be prevented. These study animals were asymptomatic by the time they reached their maturity, which in the Shar-Pei is around one year of age. For this reason, the researcher proposed that the congenital variety may be due to an immaturity of the nerve and/or muscle fibers that serve the esophagus area. Unfortunately, this same researcher did not have similar success with acquired megaesophagus. Those study animals did not grow out of the condition and eventually died of complications. Unfortunately, other researchers have not had the same optimistic results even with congenital megaesophagus. In fact, most of their animals with either AA or IME succumbed to pneumonia well before they reached maturity.

Surgical correction of the dilated esophageal portion and any impeding tissue is the only current remedy. It should be done as early as possible since the dog's progressively debilitated state makes him an increasingly poor surgical risk. In general, most animals show a marked improvement if they can survive the corrective procedures.

HIATAL HERNIA

Hiatal hernia occurs in cats and all breeds of dogs including the Shar-Pei. The term refers to tissue that abnormally protrudes through the opening where the esophagus traverses the diaphragm. There appears to be no sex-linked or breed-size predisposition.

The most common tissue that herniates is the stomach. Once thought to be associated with trauma, particularly automobile-related, it is now thought also to have congenital origins. The condition develops due to a weakened ligament that should firmly surround the esophagus as it passes through the diaphragm. The defect in the phrenoesophageal ligament actually allows the displacement of the lower esophagus to a position forward of the diaphragm. The combination of the weak ligament and shift of the esophagus' position creates the condition. Stomach tissue may

then be able to shift position due to the differences in pressure between the abdominal and thoracic cavities.

In this abnormal position, acids from the stomach's digestive process can flow upward into the esophagus whenever the lower esophageal sphincter opens. The acid causes an acute inflammation of the esophagus called reflux esophagitis; this typically generates the first identifying symptoms.

The most common symptoms of the disorder are recurrent vomiting and dyspnea, usually in a young animal. The dog's equivalent of ''heartburn'' may persist in between meals. Gagging, retching and drooling indicate the dog's discomfort. If esophagitis is present, the animal may have difficulty swallowing. Weight loss may be evident. Regurgitation of blood-streaked mucus is also common. Frequently, the dog may choose to remain in a sitting position in an attempt to take pressure off of the entrapped tissue.

The greatest danger of this condition is a larger portion of the stomach tissue actually moving up into the esophagus, called gastroesophageal intussusception. Life-threatening shock may ensue. This is an emergency situation and requires *immediate* attention!!

Diagnosis of hiatal hernia may be difficult since the condition can come and go as the tissue shifts position; however, most animals exhibit chronic symptoms. While radiographs are helpful, the best method of diagnosis is a fluoroscopy of barium moving down the esophageal tract.

Surgical repair is the treatment of choice. The latest technique entails narrowing of the enlarged diaphragmatic opening, restructuring of the phrenoesophageal ligaments, and resting the esophagus by feeding with a gastrostomy tube for five days. In most cases, these animals respond well to the corrective therapy.

A breath-taking adult Shar-Pei. Yao'Shu's Lapsang. Owner: Chuck and Margery Denton. Margery Denton, photo.

The peaceful sleep of health. Yao'Shu's Blossom X Lynch's Playboy Ho Wun II puppies. Margery Denton, photo.

CHAPTER SEVEN

DIGESTIVE DISORDERS

MALABSORPTION

Malabsorption syndrome is a complex collection of interconnected defects or disorders that ultimately lead to faulty uptake of nutrients from the small intestine. It is an area that in the past few years has begun to receive attention from researchers. As studies continue, it is becoming more and more obvious that malabsorption cannot be easily classified as having a simple or straight-forward etiology.

In order to adequately grasp the problems of this syndrome, the normal mechanism of digestion should be understood. Even as food substances arrive in the stomach, digestion has already begun by enzymes present in the dog's saliva. Once in the stomach, food elements are further broken down into their more fundamental components in order to be assimilated by the body. As this now semi-solid matter is released into the small intestine, more intense enzymatic action begins. Not only are

STOMACH

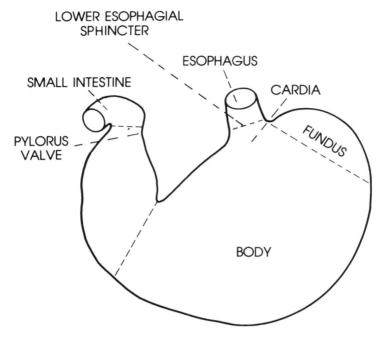

LOWER ESOPHAGIAL
SPHINCTER

ESOPHAGUS

SMALL INTESTINE

CARDIA

PYLORUS
VALVE

FUNDUS

BODY

Canine Stomach.

major enzymes present in the lumen of the intestine provided by the pancreas and the liver, but minor enzymes exist along the small, finger-like projections, called villi, that protrude from the intestinal walls. Each specialized enzyme acts on its target: protein, carbohydrate, or fat. As these food molecules are reduced to their most basic components, the protein and carbohydrate components attach to a "transfer" substance which carries them into the villi and then into the intestine's deeper tissues, where they are absorbed by the capillaries. Fat molecules do not need a carrier and are able to migrate into the deeper tissues via the lymph vessels. This process of break-down and absorption is the fundamental method by which the body is able to utilize the food it consumes.

Defects in the enzymatic-digestive mechanism or the intestinal wall ab-

sorptive structures can create an all-encompassing breakdown in vital nutrition. Unless the breakdown/uptake process is executed exactly, the body is unable to utilize food substances. This in turn generates a physical condition in the dog that is generally termed as "unthrifty." Weakened, these animals are at risk for other opportunistic diseases. Furthermore, they are poor candidates for any surgical procedure due to their low blood protein levels.

Specifically, a dog with malabsorption can display a whole battery of symptoms that may be either acutely evident or intermittently chronic. Since this disorder is confined to the small intestine and pancreas, the bowel symptoms can include: large, bulky or watery stools that may be normal or slightly more frequent; dark colored stool, vomiting, and marked weight loss may be present; pendulous abdomen, halitosis, and general malaise are common. Borborygmus, or rumbling of the stomach, is frequently heard. The pancreas' influence can create an increased fat content in the stool causing pale, voluminous, and foul smelling feces. (These signs are in marked contrast to large intestinal problems which are characterized by urgency, tenesmus, mucous and fresh blood in the stool.)

More subtle signs of the syndrome may include altered blood levels of albumin and calcium. Anemia is often found as the absorption of iron and B_{12} is affected. If protein metabolism is altered, signs of hypothyroidism may be present as protein is required for the transfer of the hormone within the blood stream. (See Hypothyroidism) Some animals have also been known to display skin disorders in association with malabsorption. The exact relationship at this time is unknown but may relate to the resulting malnutrition.

The causes of malabsorption can be 1) infiltrative such as a tumor or idiopathic inflammation of the intestinal wall, 2) abnormalities of the intestinal enzymatic-digestive process, 3) infections by fungi, bacteria or parasites, 4) dietary intolerances or allergy, or 5) extensive surgical removal of the intestine. To complicate matters, more than one of the above causes can be concurrently present. Some researchers have proposed that heredity may play a significant role in the predisposition for the underlying causes of this condition.

The most common cause of malabsorption in dogs, including the Shar-Pei, according to Dr. Peter Giger at the University of Pennsylvania, is a defect in the tissues at the base of the intestinal villi. There, due to edema, food molecules are less able to pass through the villi for assimilation by the capillaries. The exact reason for this change in the physical characteristic of the intestinal lining is unknown. Unfortunately the only method of determining the exact

Shar-Pei at 15 months of age.

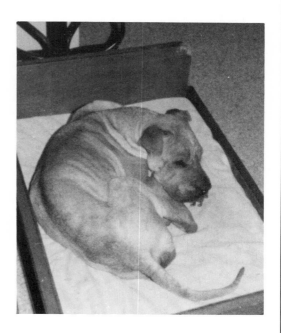

Same dog after developing malabsorption. Note severe weight loss.

type of inflammatory process is by surgical biopsy.

In some animals a digestive process defect may be due to a deficit in pancreatic enzymes, bile and/or other enzymes located along the edges of the tiny villi. Here too the exact cause for a decrease in their levels is unknown. Recently a new test called TL1 has been developed that can determine if the dog's pancreatic function is sufficient. Similarly, bile levels can be accurately determined by laboratory testing. However, tests for the levels of villi enzymes are not readily available since they are a new field of research.

Some cases of malabsorption have been connected to the increased proliferation of intestinal bacteria, fungi or parasites. Their overwhelming presence can lead to interference with absorption of carbohydrates, B_{12}, and fat metabolism. Testing for parasites and culturing for organisms is considered routine. And finally, dietary intolerances particularly to lactose have been associated with malabsorption. Diet testing for the offending substance is possible. (See Food Allergy)

In the past few years very complex, sophisticated tests have been developed to try to pin-point the exact location of the disorder. In most cases, these tests must be conducted by a specialist in the gastro-intestinal field. At this particular time, while accurate, they are very costly and time consuming.

Treatment of malabsorption, depending on the cause, may at best be difficult. Parasitic infestation is the most easily addressed. (See Health Parameters) Bacterial over-growth can be treated with a broad-spectrum antibiotic effective against anerobes. e.g. tetracycline, ampicillin, chloramphenicol, clindamycin, erythromycin, lincomycin, or penicillin. Pancreatic enzyme deficiency can be corrected by the administration of Viokase, a digestive enzyme replacement. Lactose intolerance is best treated by removal of all milk products from the animal's diet. Steroids can be effective in treating several forms of intestinal inflammation.

Dietary measures however, constitute the major avenue for medical control of malabsorption. Most practitioners suggest that, in addition to the above special measures, the dog's food be restricted to a high-protein, high-carbohydrate, low fat diet. (Hill's dog food company manufactures a special food, called "RD," that meets these requirements.) In addition, in order to fill the dog's caloric/fat needs, medium-chain triglycerides, or MCT, should be added to the daily intake. This substance can be readily purchased from a pharmacy and is simply added to the dog's ration. A good quality vitamin and mineral supplement should also be given daily. In general, the dog should be fed small meals at least three or four times daily.

Malabsorption is a complex disease process that requires prompt and thorough medical attention. If the dog is allowed to become debilitated, the prognosis for treatment is poor. Researchers are hopeful that in the next few years more concrete information about cause(s) of the disease will be available for the Shar-Pei owner. This data is desperately needed if, in fact, the condition does have a hereditary link.

GASTRIC DILATATION-TORSION

For all the breeders polled, bloat or gastric dilatation-torsion (GDT), is the most feared canine medical emergency. Occurring within minutes or hours after eating, bloat is a life-threatening situation with mortality rates as high as 68%. According to one study, aggressive medical and/or surgical intervention must be initiated within 30 to 120 minutes after *symptoms begin* in order to save the dog!

The term gastric torsion actually refers to two components that must jointly occur in order to create the syndrome. The first, gastric dilatation, or over-distention of the stomach, must be present. In itself gastric dilatation is not an ominous condition. Often found in the young puppy from over-eating and the adult from post-eating exercise, the condition can self-resolve if the stomach contents are able to escape by vomiting, burping or passing into the intestines. If, however, stomach gases are not able to, or are delayed in their escape, it sets the stage for the final requirement of torsion or twisting of the stomach around its entry and exit points. These two conditions, the trapping of excess food and gas and the twisting of the stomach, compose the condition known as gastric torsion.

What causes this combination of conditions is currently unknown. Over the years the various theories that have been proposed all seem to have a bearing on the condition, but they do not comprise the complete picture. It was first thought that the gastric over-distention was caused by the release of gases as food was digested. It has now been proven that stomach gases are actually atmospheric or "room" air, not the by-products of food breakdown. In fact, gaseous distention of the stomach can even occur in an animal which is fasting! Active air swallowing by the dog appears to be the primary source and is thought to be caused by rapid eating, excitement, fear or energetic activity.

Another theory was that feeding of certain food products, such as soybean meal, or certain forms of food, such as dry dog chow, could lead to bloat. It was believed that these foods or their form altered the rate at which they were digested. A delay in the digestion process might create the potential for over-dilation and resulting torsion. This theory has also been disproven by numerous research studies. A University of Florida study clearly indicates that the form of food has no impact on the speed with which the food moves through the digestive tract—regardless if it was canned, meat-based, dry, or moistened-dry. Similarly, soybean meal has not been conclusively associated with the bloat complex. (In the Shar-Pei, however, since they have a tendency to allergic reaction to soy products, avoidance of this food item is still recommended.) Of the studies to date, increased fat consumption appears to be the only food item that actually slows digestion, but a connection between fat levels and bloat has *not* been made.

Another theory that has had popular acclaim is limitation of the size of the meals and provision of multiple feedings within a 24 hour period. It is believed that these measures could lessen the chances of GDT. As of this time, the results of studies of this approach are inconclusive: dogs that were purposefully fed large, distending meals did not always develop the expected GDT.

Thus, no definitive evidence has been found to link a dietary cause with the occurrence of bloat. In fact, one study showed that GDT can occur in animals whether or not they are fed free-choice, meat or cereal, with or without soybean meal, or large or small quantities. Researchers are now questioning that a multiple combination of physical and environmental factors, including diet, must be present concurrently.

Originally thought to be a condition of only the large, deep-chested breeds such as the Great Dane, German Shepherds, Saint Bernards, Labrador Retrievers, Irish Setters, Irish Wolfhounds, Great Pyrenees, Boxers, Weimaraners, Old English Sheepdogs, Bloodhounds, Standard Poodles, and Doberman Pinschers, bloat has also been found in the Dachshund, Pekingese, English Bulldog and Shar-Pei. In fact the cat, fox, mink, rabbit, guinea pig, mouse, and monkey all are susceptible.

It was also once thought that there was a higher tendency for males to develop the condition than females; however, more recent studies have indicated no sexual correlation. In both sexes, the typical dog is between two and ten years of age. And, unless surgically corrected, the condition tends to recur. In addition, some lines within a breed appear to have a higher than normal tendency for the condition. Although a direct hereditary link has not been determined, most breeders would be wise to consider a familial tendency should the condition appear in their animals. A hereditary predisposition is only logical if body conformation and/or digestive defect are implicated in the condition's etiology.

In the normal dog the esophagus enters at a point at the top of the stomach organ. This upper gastric end is controlled by a sphincter which prevents the stomach's contents from going back up into the esophagus. The lower end of the stomach joins with the small intestines and has a valve which keeps the food contents in the stomach until it is ready to pass into the intestines. The stomach is held in proper position by a number of ligaments. Lying along the right side of the stomach is the spleen. The stomach normally has a great ability to expand according to the amount of food items ingested; this characteristic in fact may be the fundamental root of the bloat problem since over-filling of the stomach is so readily possible.

The prevalent philosophy is that the complex of gastric torsion seems to be dependent on the multi-presence of dilation of the stomach, slowed emptying of food contents, relaxation of the stomach's supporting structures, and excessive swallowing of air. It is believed that the combination of these factors allow the rotation of the stomach around its esophageal and intestinal "anchor points."

The exact impact of the physical characteristics of the dog is presently receiving attention. This theory proposes that the anatomical position and/or shape of the stomach and supporting structures may in fact be an essential pre-condition for bloat. If the support structures do not hold the stomach firmly in place, movement of the organ can occur with any over-filling of the stomach, triggering a dilatation-torsion response.

The supportive ligaments, weakened by chronic over-distention or physiological defect, can no longer maintain the stomach in its normal position. Over-filled, the fundus rotates, twisting the two stomach valves closed and thereby preventing the escape of food, fluid, or gas. This blockage furthers increases the stomach's dimensions as normal digestive secretions continue. Particularly in the deep-chested breeds, the gastric shift can be dramatic, causing alterations in the position of the spleen and near-by major blood vessels.

This shift in the internal organs generates the all-encompassing medical crisis. The abnormally positioned stomach encroaches on the respiratory organs, leading to a decrease in respiratory function. Infringement on major blood vessels causes a decrease in blood and oxygen to the stomach and spleen causing tissue death. This pressure on the major vessels decreases the total circulating blood volume, alters the heart's functioning, and can cause hypovolemic-like shock. Shock affects the functioning of the kidneys, intestines, and pancreas. This change in circulation also alters the physical properties of the blood, in turn creating a condition called D.I.C. or disseminated intravascular coagulation, a serious medical condition in its own right. The body's now radically unbalanced internal chemistry can cause heartbeat alterations, leading to complete heart failure and death.

This syndrome occurs rapidly, without warning, and in a previously healthy animal. Early signs that the dog is in trouble can include restlessness, whining, open-mouthed panting, frequent swallowing, retching without production, and drooling. Abdominal distention develops that has a drum-like note when tapped with a finger. As the condition worsens, signs of shock will appear: the pulse is weak and rapid, respirations are rapid and shallow, the inside of the mouth may turn pale or bluish, and the capillary refill time is slow. Eventually the animal collapses and is moribund. The owner must take measures to get the animal to veterinary care at the first sign of trouble, regardless of the hour of day or night. THIS IS AN EXTREME EMERGENCY! TIME IS OF THE ESSENCE!

Treatment of bloat focuses on relieving the over-distention of the stomach and counteracting the effects of shock. Of primary concern is the condition of shock and its impact on the heart's function. In order to treat shock an intravenous catheter will be inserted and solutions given to increase the circulating blood volume. Medications will be given to help the body to readjust its chemical balance. Steroids are frequently used to help the dog combat the shock. Once the animal is stabilized, then treatment of the underlying conditions can be instituted.

Radiographs are the most accurate method available to determine the presence of bloat. In the X-ray, the altered position of stomach and spleen can be readily seen. However, the dog must be completely stable before putting the animal through the stress of X-rays.

Historically, torsion was determined by whether or not the veterinarian could pass a rubber gastric tube into the stomach. It was thought that if the stomach had twisted, a tube would not be able to enter the stomach past the sphincter. However, it has been found that bloat can be present, and life-threatening, even though a tube can enter the stomach. In fact, one of the first measures the vet will take is to pass a tube to decompress the over-distended stomach. If this is successful, then the condition can be more readily handled as the threat of further torsion is lessened.

If a tube cannot be passed, and the dog is too unstable for surgery, a more intensive technique can be employed. In this case, a large-bore needle is inserted through the abdominal wall into the fundus of the stomach. Trapped gas will then be able to escape and pressure on the other internal structures lessened. A gastric tube may then be passed. Although effective, this procedure, called gastrocentesis, carries with it the chance of gastric contents leaking into the abdomen. A resulting peritonitis, or inflammation of the abdominal lining, is possible and is a serious condition requiring aggressive medical care. For this reason, gastrocentesis is not initially used except in the extreme emergency.

Once the critical stage has been successfully managed, the underlying cause(s) of bloat can be addressed. Surgical procedures are employed in an attempt to prevent the condition from recurring. In animals that are not surgically corrected, 80% of the dogs have a further episode, most having fatal outcomes. Although emergency surgery itself carries some risk, with a 40% average mortality rate, it is still significantly less than the relative risk of non-treatment.

Currently there are two approaches to surgical treatment: prevention of gastric retention, which includes alteration of the control-valves of the stomach, and prevention of the stomach from altering its position. Since the role of the stomach valves in bloat has not been clearly defined, most practitioners focus their attention to anchoring the stomach in its normal anatomical position.

One method used to confine the stomach's movement is tube gastrostomy. A gastric tube is placed through the external abdominal wall and sutured into the stomach. As the incision heals, adhesions "tie" the stomach to the abdominal wall and prevent the stomach from twisting. Another popular method is called circumcostal gastropexy. In this technique a layer of outer stomach tissue is wrapped around the 11th or 12th rib and tacked back down onto the stomach wall. This "restraining strap" prevents any movement of the stomach should it over-distend. Recent data indicates that the strength of the adhesions of a circumcostal gastropexy is approximately twice that of tube gastrostomy when examined 0 to 100 days postoperatively. In addition, the success rate of gastropexy is indicated by only 15% of the dogs having a recurrence of bloat after the procedure.

Post-operative care involves careful monitoring of the dog for gastric and cardiac complications. As the dog improves, his diet is slowly advanced from sips of water to bland food given every few hours. Antibiotics are generally administered to prevent post-operative infections.

The prognosis for affected animals is greatly improved with the newer techniques for management of shock and surgery. It is important, however, that the owner be ever conscious of the need for moderation in the care of these animals. In general, research data indicates that there *are* some preventative measures. Animals should be fed frequent, small meals of moistened food. The quantity of daily food should be closely calculated. In no case should they be allowed to over-drink either before or after a meal. Some breeders have had good success by raising the food and water bowls to the dog's chest level. This appears to decrease the amount of air swallowing as the dog feeds. Exercise should be strictly limited around feeding time: food should not be offered four to six hours before and approximately one hour after exercise. And above all, at the first sign of distress immediate veterinary assistance should be obtained.

CHAPTER EIGHT

INFERTILITY DISORDERS

INFERTILITY

Infertility, regardless of the sex of the animal, can be one of the most frustrating and obscure condition for the hopeful breeder and veterinarian alike. The inter-relatedness of medical conditions, the impact of seemingly minor influences, and even the psychological component of the animal and breeding event make infertility evaluation a time-consuming and tedious ordeal.

In order for the owner and breeder to best understand the systematic approach most often used by the veterinarian, this chapter will deal with the most common conditions influencing the male and the female. It should be noted, however, that a combination of events or conditions may be present concurrently, therefore making diagnosis even more difficult.

The end results of a successful mating: Xanadu Intuition with lovely cream litter. Helen Armacost, owner/breeder.

Infertility in the Male:

In the male animal there exist at least nine different medical conditions that can predispose to infertility. In reference to the psychological aspects, it should be noted that many dogs who have been previously discouraged from interest in a female by their owner may exhibit mating difficulty. This is especially true in households where intact females are in close proximity to the stud male. Young males are especially sensitive to this sort of correction and may need multiple exposures and enthusiastic encouragement in order to succeed. Presenting a female to a young male before he is physically mature may in effect create future failures since confusion may become associated with the mating event.

It has also been shown that both viral and bacterial infections can directly influence the fertility of the male. A bacterium called *Brucella canis* is the most frequent infection causing male infertility. This organism causes inflammation of the epididymis (seminal duct) and testicles. Transmission is by sexual

---

CAUSES OF INFERTILITY IN THE MALE

- *psychological factors preventing mating*
- *decrease or arrest of sperm production*
- *infection*
- *testicular disorders*
- *penis and prepuce disorders*
- *prostate disorders*
- *sexual overactivity*
- *inbreeding*
- *congenital reproductive abnormalities*

---

contact, ingestion of vaginal discharge, and in some cases from in-utero infections. It is *extremely* contagious and requires lengthy and expensive antibiotic treatment. Cure is not always possible. Similarly, the distemper and herpes viruses have been associated with infertility in the dog.

Testicular injury is another cause of infertility. Dog fights, automobile accidents, or excessive heat to the scrotum can all lead to this result, as can tumors, prostatitis, inguinal hernias, and undescended testicles. Injuries to the penis or prepuce may be painful and may ultimately discourage the male.

The aging process may also have its impact on the production and/or quality of sperm produced. Some studies have shown that even in proven males, the amount of sperm decreases between two and seven years of age. The cause of this condition, called spermatogenic arrest or testicular atrophy, is unknown but is considered a normal part of the aging process. Some medical conditions such as thyroiditis also affects sperm quality. In order to correctly assess the sperm-producing abilities of the male, samples should be monitored for a 6- to 12-month time span.

Recent research has indicated that close in-breeding of animals can lead to a lower conception rate, number of puppies born, and number of surviving puppies. It is believed that this may be due to the males' having a poorer quality of sperm in regard to volume, motility, and normalcy. With this information in mind, breeders need to keep accurate records on the degree of in-breeding in relation to their line's reproductive performance.

Assessment of the male in question should include a thorough history including the number of females bred, how many of the females conceived and produced surviving puppies and the frequency of use of the stud. (Overuse can lead to decreased sperm quality and quantity.) The dog's attitude toward the mating process should be discussed. Any familial disorders in the dog's line should be outlined. Conditions such as hip dysplasia, hypothyroidism, Addison's disease and any prescribed medications need to be included in the history. Cultures for *Brucella canis* and other bacteria should be conducted. In addition, a complete physical exam should be provided with any necessary laboratory evaluations; multiple semen samples will be required. Hormone level evaluation and testicular biopsy will also be included if warranted. This mass of information will help determine whether the condition is a genetic or acquired entity.

Treatment of inherited infertility has a relatively poor prognosis. Although replacement hormone therapy with testosterone, estrogen, and progesterone has been tried, its success has not been encouraging. Negative side effects are common with hormone replacement.

DOG SEMEN EVALUATION

volume	0.5-30 ml
color	milky white
normal motility	80%
cell structure	less than 20% abnormal
total sperm count	300×10^6

should be considered. In comparison to the male, the number of abnormalities influencing the female's fertility are greater and more complex due inherently to her more intricate, hormonally regulated heat or estrus cycles. It can be expected that the evaluation of the bitch will be lengthy and involved.

To begin, the infertile bitch should be tested for a *Brucella canis* infection. This infection, as in the male, is responsible for a large percentage of infertility problems. (See infertility in the male section) It can cause early, undetected fetal demise at 10-20 days, or abortion at around 50 days gestation. Transmission of the disease is by sexual contact, contact with aborted fetal tissue, and vaginal or seminal discharge. Treatment may be lengthy and expensive with the newer antibiotics available. Still, with no guarantee of success, use of these animals for breeding is unpromising.

Of recent concern is the recognition that some bitches have what is referred to as an "atypical" heat cycle. This does not mean that the cycle is abnormal or absent; rather, that it deviates from the expected pattern of normal estrus. It may be "silent" or "split" in that the usual signs are not obvious or occur at unexpected times. Atypical cycles

Hopefully the evaluations will uncover an acquired condition that is responsive to treatment or removal, and thereby return the animal to normal reproductive function.

Infertility in the Female:

Once a reproductive abnormality in the *male* has been conclusively ruled out, then conditions affecting the female usually first become evident when the bitch refuses to stand for the stud, even though she should be "ready" according to the expected time frame. It has been noted that a number of bitches deviate from the usual breeding-on-the-tenth-day routine. After the onset of vaginal bleeding, some will be receptive on the fourth day and others not until the nineteenth day. Attempting to mate according to a textbook formula can lead to reproductive failure, when in fact the bitch is quite healthy. Ultimately, the bitch's behavior toward the stud should be the deciding factor as to when to breed, although vaginal smears are also helpful.

Abnormalities of the vagina or vulva are other causes of refusal to mate. Persistent hymens and other structural impediments can be readily detected by veterinary examination. Surgical correction is available.

In addition, as in the male, psychological factors may play a role in the receptiveness and therefore the fertility of the bitch. In these cases, artificial insemination may be a reasonable alternative.

The Happy Family: a breeder's dream. Alyssa Brackenbury, breeder.

As a part of the bitch's physical evaluation, tests to rule out any underlying endocrine or hormonal deficit should be conducted. Infertility-inducing bacterial infections, endometritis, or pyometra should be addressed. Ovarian cysts, tumors, liver or adrenal disease, hypothyroidism, and pituitary disorders can all affect fertility.

Any Shar-Pei bitch that has not had a heat cycle within six months of reaching her physical maturity, as accepted for the breed, should be given a thorough medical work-up. Conversely, heat cycle irregularity should be considered part of the aging process in bitches that are eight years or older.

While some reproductive disorders are complex, most failures are due to relatively simple difficulties such as faulty timing of the mating, minor underlying bacterial infections, or over-use of the male. In these cases, correction of the causative factor(s) will return the animal to full reproductive status. If, however, the condition is due to a fundamental defect in the hormonal, structural, or genetic function of the animal, male or female, serious consideration should be given as to its suitability for breeding. As in most disorders, breeding the-best-to-the-best is the only way to assure the future health and productivity of the breed—be it the tiny Skye Terrier, the mammoth Great Dane, or the rare Shar-Pei.

A devoted Shar-Pei mother with a thriving litter. Betsy Davison, breeder.

CHAPTER NINE

BASIC CANINE HEALTH PARAMETERS

HOW TO KNOW WHEN A VETERINARIAN IS NEEDED:

Distinguishing between an "off" day and actual illness in a dog can sometimes be difficult for an owner. Frequently the signs of illness are vague and/or intermittent. In general, however, most vets would prefer that the owner bring in the animal early, before it is extremely ill, rather than waiting "to be sure."

The following common, although subtle, signs of illness require veterinary attention.

- Unexplained loss of appetite
- Weight loss or gain
- Unexplained excessive thirst
- Frequent urination, difficult urination or urinary accidents in the house
- Diarrhea or constipation
- Fever
- Abnormal breathing
- Coughing
- Vomiting or retching
- Altered behavior: depression, lethargy, agitation
- Loss of consciousness
- Evidence of pain
- Unexplained muscle shaking or twitching
- Difficulty walking or rising
- Paralysis
- Bleeding
- Broken bones
- Wounds, bites, cuts
- Squinting or discharge from the eye
- Head shaking or ear scratching
- Scratching or chewing of the skin

Owners should keep names and telephone numbers of veterinarian and emergency clinics posted clearly for all family members. As one breeder so aptly put it: "children and dogs rarely get sick during office hours!"

HOME MEDICINE CHEST:

In certain circumstances, a dog may require treatment with a human, over-the-counter medication. Having these items on hand for first aid care is advisable. However, veterinary advice should be obtained *before administration*.

Pain relief—Aspirin or Tylenol
Antacids—Di-Gel or Mylanta
Antibiotic ointment—Bacitracin
Antidiarrheal—Kaopectate
Motionsickness—Dramamine or Bonine
Antihistamine—Dristan or Allerest
Antiseptic—hydrogen peroxide or Betadine
Anti-cough—Robitussin
Laxative—Milk of Magnesia or Metamucil
Poisoning—Ipecac (to induce vomiting); Give only if instructed to do so!

Included in this kit should be:
rolled gauze bandage cottonballs
adhesive tape 10 inch piece
Q-tips of 2×4
tweezers wood for
thermometer (rectal) splinting
scissors

TAKING A TEMPERATURE:

A rectal thermometer should always be used. The thermometer should be shaken down to below 95 degrees and the silver end liberally covered with Vaseline. The thermometer can be gently inserted while the dog is in either a standing or lying position, but he should remain in that original position until the procedure is completed. The thermometer is gently inserted by placing it against the anus and applying soft pressure until it is inside the rectum for approximately two inches. If any resistance is felt, preventing the thermometer from entering or advancing, the procedure should be discontinued. Under *NO* circumstances should the thermometer be forced into place. Once in position, the thermometer should remain undisturbed for at least two minutes. The owner should maintain a firm grasp on the thermometer at all times.

If the animal is standing, he should not be allowed to sit. Holding the tail and the thermometer in the same hand will steady both dog and owner. The thermometer is then removed by gently rotating as it is withdrawn and cleaned off with Kleenex. Reading of the thermometer is best done in good lighting where the small gradations can be readily seen. Any temperature over 102.5 F. degrees should be reported to the veterinarian immediately. Aspirin should not be given to lower a dog's temperature unless directly instructed to do so by the vet.

TAKING A HEART RATE:

The easiest method for taking a heart rate is to place the dog on the floor lying on his right side. The heartbeat can then be readily felt by placing the fingers (not the thumb) on the dog's chest just behind his top "elbow." The normal rate for a resting, relaxed dog is between 70 and 120 beats per minute. If the animal is restless, counting for 15 seconds and then multiplying by four will give a fairly accurate rate.

TAKING A RESPIRATORY RATE:

The dog's respiratory rate varies radically depending on the temperature, his activity level and his emotional state. The only accurate picture can be obtained with the resting animal.

As the dog inhales, the lungs fill and the ribs expand with a noticeable rise of the chest. As the dog exhales, the lungs empty out air, the ribs return to their normal position and the chest falls. Counting the rise of the chest as the dog inhales is the most efficient means of determining the respirational rate. The owner should also note whether the breathing rate is regular or irregular, easy or strained, noisy or quiet.

If there is doubt whether the animal is breathing, a wet hand can be placed directly in front of the nostrils and any "air" noted. Another method involves placing a small mirror up against the nostrils and checking to see if the mirror fogs from the warm, moist breath. Any absence of breath is a SEVERE medical emergency and artificial resuscitation should be commenced immediately.

HOW TO COLLECT A URINE SAMPLE:

The most accurate picture of the dog's renal status is a sample of the last half of the first urination of the morning. It should be caught in a clean glass or plastic container. Having the animal on a leash simplifies the procedure.

Samples from female dogs are acquired by approaching her slowly from the rear. As she squats to void, a small amount should be allowed to escape before sliding a low-profile container beneath her. Most animals are unaware that they are voiding into the container and not on the ground. As she stands, the container can be safely moved away from her.

A urine sample from a male dog is acquired by allowing the dog to lift his leg and void a small amount. While he is still urinating, a wide-mouthed, deep container, such as a clean mayonnaise jar, is moved under his leg to catch the urine. In some cases the use of two people is easier, as one can handle the leash and the other can collect the specimen. Care should be taken that as he lowers his leg the collection container is not touched. This technique may require agility and practice on the part of the owner. Be prepared to have wet hands after the first few attempts!

Needless to say, urine collection should not be attempted when the owner is rushed. Many animals are quite shy about their voiding habits and may be reluctant to oblige when the owner is hovering in anticipation.

Urine samples should be clearly labeled with the dog's and owner's names. Samples should be examined immediately or refrigerated for no more than three hours. If the sample is more than three hours old, then another sample should be obtained. For many owners obtaining the sample immediately outside of the vet's office is the most accurate and efficient method.

HOW TO COLLECT
A STOOL SAMPLE:

Collection of fecal material is fairly straightforward. A fresh sample should be acquired and placed in a plastic or glass container. Some vet clinics provide tiny plastic, zip-lock baggies for the transport of feces. Any sample should be labeled with the dog and owner's name and the test requested. Any blood or mucus seen by the owner should be clearly noted on the container's label.

Samples should be examined immediately or refrigerated for no more than twelve hours. If the sample is allowed to ''sit,'' some varieties of worm eggs will disintegrate and be undetectable, rendering a false-negative test result.

"Following in Dad's footsteps." Betsy Davison, owner/breeder.

NORMAL PARAMETERS:

In some cases, for simplicity, technical units of measure have been omitted as they are standard in the industry.
Temperature: (adult) 100 to 102.5 degrees Fahrenheit rectally
(puppy) 101 to 103 degrees Fahrenheit rectally

Heart beat: (adult) 100-130 per minute
(puppy) 130-169 per minute

Respirations: (adult) 22-28 per minute
(puppy) 26-30 per minute

Normal Blood Values per evaluation sample (noting that slight variations may be used by individual laboratories):

hemaglobin	12-18
hematocrit	37-55
red blood cells	5.5-8.5
white blood cells	6.0-17.0
platelets	2-9

Normal Blood Chemistry per evaluation sample (slight variations may be used by individual laboratories):

Urea nitrogen	10-20
Glucose	70-100
Calcium	8-12
Potassium	3.5-5.5
Phosphorus	2-5
Sodium	135-150
Magnesium	2-5
Chloride	100-115

Capillary Refill Time: approximately 1-1.5 seconds.

Find an area in the mouth that is not pigmented (pink). In the Shar-Pei it may be over a tooth or on the inside of the upper lip. Press firmly for one second, then count: "1001, 1002 . . ." When the pink color returns, that is the capillary refill time.

Normal Urine values (slight variations may be used by individual laboratories):

volume	24-41 millimeters per kilogram of weight per day
pH	6-7
specific gravity	1.018-1.050
protein	0-trace
glucose	0-trace

HOW TO GIVE A PILL:

Training a dog to accept a pill graciously should be started as a young puppy. Oral medications can rapidly become an area of conflict between owner and animal. For this reason, it is far easier to convince a reluctant puppy to swallow a pill than it is a struggling, mature, 50 pound Shar-Pei! Since almost every animal will require medicating by pill form within his lifetime, this early training is important.

Beginning slowly and gently, the owner places the dog in a standing or sitting position, facing in the direction so that the owner's dominant hand (right or left) will be placing the pill into the mouth. The other hand then tilts the dog's head upward to a 45 degree angle by softly grasping the top of the muzzle. The upper lips are pushed down into the dog's mouth and over the upper teeth by the owner's fingers. The dominant hand holds the pill between forefinger and thumb and the remaining fingers push downward on the dog's lower jaw. As the jaw opens, the pill is quickly placed as far back into the center of the mouth as possible and the fingers removed. Close the dog's mouth and gently but firmly hold it closed, while allowing the head to return to a level position. Soft downward massage of the throat will encourage the dog to swallow. Most dogs will indicate they are swallowing by a slight protrusion of the tongue.

The process should be approached with a calm and matter-of-fact attitude. Many animals naturally fear an object being forced into their mouths. A second person to steady the dog's hindquarters may be necessary until the animal realizes he will not be injured. As the animal becomes more adept at this technique, the muzzle can be allowed to slightly open to facilitate swallowing. Young puppies and most adults soon learn that, if they cooperate, the procedure will be quickly and painlessly over. The goal is to be able to medicate the animal with a minimum of stress.

For aggressive or untrained dogs hiding the pill in a food item may be an alternative method. It should be noted, however, that many dogs become wise to this approach and will eat the treat and spit out the pill! Mixing the medication within the daily meal is usually not recommended since the dog may refuse to eat knowing the medicine is present.

HOW TO GIVE A LIQUID:

To administer a liquid medication requires the same initial approach as does pill administration. The dog is standing or sitting in the proper position with his head in a normal position. The dominant hand holds the medication while the other hand controls the head.

In this case, however, care should be taken that the medicine is in a non-breakable container, such as a plastic medicine dropper or newer pediatric medicine ''spoon.'' Under no circumstances should the container be made of glass in case the dog should bite down. In addition, the container should have only the *exact amount* required for that particular dose. Pouring the medication directly out of a multi-dose bottle into the dog's mouth is *strongly discouraged*. The dog can receive more or less than the prescribed dose and can, if struggling, choke on a large, accidentally splashed amount.

With liquid medications the dog's mouth is held closed by the opposite hand, holding the muzzle and the lower jaw. The dominant hand separates the dog's lips and gently pushes the medicine dropper in behind the large canine, or "eye," teeth. The fluid is squeezed or poured slowly into the mouth, small amounts at a time.

Most animals do not seem to object to a liquid medication being given as much as a pill. However, the use of two persons can simplify the technique as the second person can steady the hindquarters.

HOW TO GIVE EYE MEDICATION:

Eye medications may be easily instilled by placing the animal in a standing or sitting position. The eye medication is held firmly in the dominant hand. The dog's head is steadied by the other hand, while the lower fingers or palm of the dominant hand gently pull down the lower eyelid. The ointment or solution is squeezed into the pouch made by the lower lid and the eyeball. Once an adequate amount is in place, the eyelid is allowed to return to its normal position. The medication will disperse across the eye as the animal blinks.

Caution must be taken when applying eye medications which are in small tubes with metal "snouts." If the animal should suddenly jump, the metal can severely injure the eye. Keeping the tube a safe distance while close enough to "hit the target" is a process of trial and error. With many dogs the cheeks will at first be wearing more of the medication than the eye! This should be expected, especially if the eye condition is particularly painful or the animal is unusually sensitive. Any increase in redness, inflammation, irritation or discharge from the eye should be reported to the veterinarian immediately.

Any and all medications used in the eye should be specifically labeled *ophthalmologic*. This indicates that special care was taken by the pharmaceutical company to keep the drug clear of any substance that might cause injury or irritation to the eye. Under no circumstances should medications be used that are not made especially for the eye or if the drug is out of date. (Most medications have an expiration date stamped onto the end or body of the container.) If there is any doubt, do NOT use it! If the container is contaminated by contact with skin or hair from either the owner or the dog, wipe the applicator's tip with alcohol, squeeze a small amount out, and wipe again with alcohol. The applicator's tip must be clean at all times!

HOW TO GIVE EAR MEDICATION:

See Stenotic canals and Otitis Externa.

Shu Tzao Rust'in at Changa, six months old. Changa Kennels.

WORMING: TYPES, TESTING, TREATMENT

Roundworms:

Roundworm eggs can exist for years in soil from where the dog accidentally ingests them after contaminating his paws. The eggs hatch in the intestines and the larvae migrate to the lungs via the blood system. The larvae then are coughed up and swallowed into the stomach again. The pup may frequently gag and cough during this stage of the worm's development. Once back in the intestines, they mature into the adult form, reaching a length of one to seven inches. The female worm can lay thousands of eggs in a 24 hour period.

If pregnant, the female dog can transmit the worm infestation to her puppies in utero and while nursing. For this reason, all bitches should be wormed prior to mating, puppies should be tested after birth, and all dogs routinely wormed throughout life.

Roundworms are transmissible to humans although they do not reach maturity within the human body. Human infestations cause fever, anemia, liver enlargement, pneumonia, and general malaise as the larvae migrate through the body tissues.

Testing is by fecal examination. Treatment consists of pyrantelpamoate (Nemex, Strongoid T) given orally. Three weeks after the final dose a repeat stool sample should be evaluated to determine if the animal is worm-free. Some breeders who show their animals or who are in frequent contact with other dogs, routinely worm their adult dogs every six months.

Hookworms:

Hookworms are thin worms that reach a length of only ¼ to ½ inch. Its small size should not belie its potential impact on the dog-host. These worms fasten to the lining of the intestinal tract where they feed on the dog's blood. Acquired by ingestion or penetration of the skin, puppies may become infested from the mother's milk. On rare occasions, for young puppies, hookworm infestation can be life-threatening. Even adult dogs can become anemic and dehydrated with continuous diarrhea.

Humans are susceptible to hookworm if they come in contact with it in the soil. The hookworm larva is able to penetrate a man's skin and will migrate, causing long itchy streaks.

Diagnosis is obtained by fecal examination. Treatment consists of Stongoid T given orally. For young puppies, more intensive medical treatment and support, such as blood transfusions, may be required. A repeated stool examination should be done three weeks after completion of the treatment.

Whipworms:

Whipworms are white, thread-thin worms that infest the large intestine and feed off of the dog's blood. Affected animals will have diarrhea, dull coats, and loss of weight. Symptoms may be vague and intermittent.

Diagnosis is made by visualization of the egg from a stool sample. Repeated samples may be needed since worms may be present in the intestine but periodically fail to shed eggs in the stool. Treatment is provided by fenbendazole (Panacur). Repeated stool specimens should be examined every three months in areas of the country where the worms are numerous.

Tapeworms:

Two forms of tapeworm can infest the dog. One is carried by the common flea and the other by the rabbit or mouse. The dog acquires the worm by ingesting the flea or the internal organs of infected cattle, rabbits or mice. The worm is carried into the dog's intestines where it attaches to the wall. As the worm develops, its body divides into segments which allows the worm to attain lengths of several feet. These segments also contain the worm's eggs; as they break off from the body of the worm, the segment and eggs are passed out with the feces. When fresh, they are flat, white and capable of movement, when dry the segments appear like grains of rice, approximately ¼ inch in length.

Diagnosis requires the visualization of segments in the stool. The entire worm must be eliminated or the worm will regenerate. Symptoms of the infestation are usually unremarkable with only a change in the quality of the dog's coat or a minor weight loss as evidence.

Tapeworm infestations can be transmitted to man by ingesting a flea or dog feces. Children are most susceptible to this condition. Infestation of an adult usually involves the dog grooming the rectal area and then their coat; as the adult strokes the coat, his hand is contaminated. The worm can cause damage to the human's liver, lungs and brain.

Prevention consists of aggressive flea control and preventing access to raw meat and hunting of rodents. Treatment is by administering praziquantil (Droncit). Reinfestation is possible if the dog again has access to the carrier-host.

Heartworms:

Heartworm is becoming an increasingly severe problem throughout the country. Once confined mostly to the more temperate regions, the heartworm is present in every state, including Alaska and Hawaii.

The heartworm microfilariae circulate within the dog's blood stream. A mosquito bites the dog and absorbs the microfilariae with the blood "meal." The microfilariae reach a second maturational stage within the mosquito within two weeks. The mosquito then bites a second dog and, as he does so, some of the larvae passively escape from the flea's saliva into the dog. Here, in the dog's skin, the larvae remain for 90 to 120 days. Eventually they migrate by way of the blood stream to the right side of the heart and adjacent blood vessels where they take up residence. Within five months the larvae have matured into adult heartworms. The females ultimately deliver immature microfilariae into the blood which is then accessible to passing mosquito bites. The cycle begins again.

In advanced cases, the worms so compromise the blood circulation that pulmonary hypertension and heart failure may occur. In the early stages, the dog displays signs of coughing, weight loss, and exercise intolerance. Diagnosis is usually made by examining a blood sample for the presence of microfilariae.

The dog may have heartworms without microfilariae being detectable. In 10-30% of the heartworm cases, it has been found that the worms are either of one sex or sterile. In that case, no "offspring" would be detectable in the blood. Another test, can now determine the presence of a heartworm antigen in the dog's blood which is present regardless of the sexual characteristics of the worm. It is apparently only 80% accurate in diagnosing adult heartworm and therefore must be interpreted in light of other clinical signs.

Prevention is possible by administering a medication which prevents the larvae from passing through the maturational stages. By giving a daily dose, according to the weight of the dog, of Nemacide, Pet-Dec or Filaribits (diethlycarbamazine citrate), the dog is adequately protected. The medication must, however, be given religiously *EACH DAY* in order for all of the larvae to be destroyed. All of these methods must be continued while the mosquito is in the environment and two months beyond: in the northern states from April until December, in the southern states year around.

A new product, Heartguard 30 or ivermectin, has just been made available to veterinarians. It is given orally, according to the dog's weight, on a once-monthly schedule. As of this time, it is approved for use in all breeds at the normal dosage; however, Collies and Collie-X's have displayed a poor response to high doses of the drug. It would be wise to observe any rare breed, including the Shar-Pei, for an untoward reaction while on a newly available medication.

Once a dog has contracted heartworms, the disease may progress without detection until far advanced. It may be possible to save the dog by following an aggressive medical regime. If microfilariae are detected in the blood screening test, then an exact laboratory confirmation should be done, called an microfilariae I.D. test. Here the lab will measure the microfilariae's width to be positive that this is the offspring of the heartworm.

If the test is positive, then the dog will be treated with an arsenic-related compound, called Caparsolate. This drug kills the adult worms that are encroaching the heart. The dog must be watched closely over the two days' series of injections as this drug is highly toxic to the liver. In addition, the dog must be kept very quiet and on restricted exercise for three to five weeks in order to prevent a clump of dead worms from breaking off and floating in the blood stream; a free-floating clump could potentially block a major blood vessel and possibly cause pulmonary tissue damage, hemorrhage, and death. After the adult worms have been destroyed, the microfilariae must be treated. At about four to five weeks, Levamisole is given orally at home. This will continue for seven days when a repeat blood test will be done. If microfilariae are still present, Levamisole will be continued for another five days. The final step is to then place these animals on preventative oral treatment.

Since the long-term risk of heartworm is permanent damage to the heart and lungs, with possible death, the saying "an ounce of prevention is worth a pound of cure" is especially appropriate.

CHAPTER TEN

CARE OF THE GERIATRIC SHAR-PEI

The aging process is an inevitable part of life. Eventually the exuberance of youth is replaced with the silvered dignity of age. As the old companion moves into that phase, the Shar-Pei owner may need to re-think some of his care that has become automatic over the course of years.

The average Shar-Pei owner can expect to have his dog's company into the double-digit years. Information on the Shar-Pei's longevity comes from

CALCULATING THE AGE OF YOUR DOG

Age of Dog	Age of Human
1	13
2	20
3	25
4	30
5	35
6	40
7	45
8	50
9	55
10	60
11	65
12	70
13	75
14	80

the news is encouraging that even on this side of the ocean Shar-Pei thrive a decade or more.

Veterinarians consider medium-sized dogs such as the Shar-Pei to be senior citizens at approximately eight years and older. It is at this stage that the abundant vitality of the mature animal begins the physiological decline of the older dog. Internal and external physical changes influence the dog's quality of life. Proper care can help to mollify these changes and becomes increasingly important as the years go by.

APPEARANCE

The physical changes associated with aging actually may begin during the younger years with white or silver hairs appearing on the muzzle. Dark-coated dogs will begin to show graying sooner than lighter dogs. This graying will slowly spread from the muzzle to encompass most of the head, forearms

breeders in Hong Kong and the few American Shar-Pei that have reached the Golden Years. Of the few that have,

A Shar-Pei moving into her Golden Years. Note the loss of muzzle size.

and front and rear paws.

In most cases, unless there exists an underlying medical condition, the amount of coat does not significantly change with age. However, the quality of the coat does change, with the hair becoming dryer and brittle to the touch. This harsh texture may precipitate hair breakage, leading to a shortening of the coat hairs rather than a decrease in the actual number of hair follicles. A reduction in skin oil production may also affect the skin's smoothness, leading to dandruff and itching. Moderate use of a good-quality, soothing dog shampoo will help to alleviate the problem. Adding one teaspoon of Alpha-Keri oil to the warm rinse water helps to soften the skin and lessen itching.

Age causes skin elasticity to slowly decrease, allowing more sag in the throat and abdominal area. In the Shar-Pei this loss of skin turgor may not be as apparent as in other breeds since wrinkles are an expected characteristic of the breed.

Grooming plays an important part in the daily care of the aging pet: on one hand it gives the owner an opportunity to assess the dog's physical and mental condition; it gives the dog the owner's undivided attention that is so comforting; and, it provides the skinfolds with daily attention to prevent minor irritations from developing into larger problems. (See Skinfold Dermatitis)

Use of flea products must be carefully chosen since the older dog is generally more sensitive to chemicals and drugs. Discussing the type and brand of flea product with your veterinarian is particularly important. Older dogs can become rapidly drug toxic since their livers may not be functioning as completely as before. A product that has been a household stand-by may actually be harmful to the older pet.

Nail care becomes extremely important as the dog's activity level decreases. The nails, ordinarily worn away from daily ambulation, rapidly become overgrown. Long nails prevent adequate footing and may lead to injuries from slips and falls. Allowed to remain too long, a nail may break off and set the stage for a serious paw infection. Trimming of the front and rear nails may need to be done on a bimonthly basis. If the animal objects to the procedure, nail filing is a suitable alternative.

HEARING

A natural part of aging, hearing loss is usually a gradual process. Some animals compensate so well that, to the owner, the realization that the dog has a hearing impairment may lead them to believe that the loss was sudden. An owner may have the first clue that hearing is compromised when an ordinarily obedient dog totally ignores a command. Important sounds, such as the owner returning home, may be completely missed. The dog may appear to be sleeping very soundly since he does not hear the owner's approach. Some animals may begin to bark excessively in response to this loss.

Hearing is the dog's best protection and any impairment is a major threat to the animal's safety. Evidence of a decrease in hearing should be taken very seriously. Hard of hearing animals should never be allowed unrestricted outdoor freedom since they can no longer hear oncoming cars or the approach of aggressive animals and other dangers.

VISION

In the elderly dog vision changes are inevitable. In many animals a white, hazy cloud will develop in the eye's lens, called lenticular sclerosis. Technically not a cataract, it shares a similar but milder physical impact, in that the quality of vision is decreased. While this condition does not cause total blindness, the animal may have difficulty negotiating at night. Thus, some owners install an inexpensive night light near the animal's bed and food bowls.

NUTRITION

As the gastric and intestinal organs age, the ability to assimilate and utilize food declines while the lowered activity level burns fewer calories. Dog foods that kept him fit and trim as a young adult begin to add unwanted pounds to the older, less mobile dog. Obesity ranks as the single most pervasive problem in the geriatric dog. As his activity level decreases, the excess calories are turned to fat; this added weight discourages further activity which in turn uses even fewer calories. The stress of obesity is a factor in many serious physical diseases, taking its toll on the heart, the joints and the kidneys.

The elderly dog has specific nutritional requirements which differ slightly from the younger dog. Older dogs need a smaller quantity of high quality protein, increased fiber to prevent constipation, decreased fat content and additional vitamins and minerals. In recent years some dog food manufactures have addressed the need to reduce the caloric intake of older dogs. To name a few good-quality brands: Purina makes "Fit and Trim," Science Diet makes "Canine Senior," and Gaines makes "Cycle 4." These manufactures have calibrated the ingredients to fit the elderly dog's dietary requirements. Whether in dry or canned form, they serve to provide the necessary intake without jeopardizing the older dog's decreasing liver and kidney function.

Many veterinarians recommend vitamin supplements for this age group. Calcium and phosphorus may be needed but should be carefully calculated according to the dog's dietary intake. Excess of some vitamins or minerals is as hazardous as a deficiency.

Feeding is best provided in smaller, more frequent meals, provided the total daily quantity is appropriate. Most dogs enjoy two meals a day, morning and evening. If the dog has arthritis, raising the dish helps the dog comfortably reach the food. A cardboard box, small stool or stand that will raise the dish to the dog's chest level allows him to feed with his weight evenly distributed on all fours.

The aging animal's appetite may not be as hearty as in his younger days. This is often due to dental problems which hinder proper chewing. Frequently the older dog has a build up of tartar that irritates the gums, providing a perfect setting for periodontal disease. The resulting bone and tissue destruction can lead to the loss of teeth and feeding problems. If the animal shows a reluctance to eat, has bad breath or tooth loss, veterinary dental care is in order. Soaking dry dog food in warm water until soft may be of help to the animal who has extensive dental involvement.

Perhaps the hardest of all changes for the loving owner is the elimination of treats. A major cause of weight problems in the older dog, it is often a significant way the owner communicates his affection to his pet. Many owners feel guilty that by removing treats the pet will feel the owner no longer cares for him. In truth, eliminating treats may be an act of totally unselfish love, if it will assist in improving the quality of the dog's life. Love and affection can and should be abundantly present for the elderly Shar-Pei, but demonstrated by time, touch and tenderness—not by a food product.

ELIMINATION

As the dog ages, kidney and bowel function begin to change. A sedentary life style, increasing joint pain, neurological deterioration, decreasing hormonal response and increasing tendency for kidney/bladder/intestinal disease all impact the dog's desire or capability to control his eliminations. The result may be a loss of bowel or bladder control, particularly at night. Called incontinence, the previously fastidious dog will arise in the morning to a soaked or soiled bedding and coat. This is not a willful act on the part of the pet, but a natural consequence of aging; however, urinary disorders should be ruled-out by the veterinarian.

Many owners address the problems of incontinence by providing a owner-supervised, late night "bathroom" outing before the family retires. Similarly, the pet should be allowed outside immediately upon awakening since control of a full bladder is tenuous. Frequent access to the outdoors during the day-time hours is mandatory. It may be noted that merely placing the dog outside does not necessarily mean that he has eliminated. In fact, he may have settled down for a snooze in a favorite location until it is time to return inside!

Providing a washable environment for the pet assists in managing the inevitable mishaps that will occur. Bath mats or toweling are more owner-convenient than cedar beds or fabric cushions. The bedding, however, should remain as thick as possible to absorb any urine as well as to provide adequate padding for the animal.

Although tempting, restricting the dog's water intake is not recommended since his kidney function is already jeopardized. In fact, an animal with impaired kidney function typically consumes greater amounts of water than an animal with normal kidneys. Removing access to water can result in the animal developing total kidney failure, which is life-threatening.

A hormone-responsive urinary incontinence is commonly found in the older, spayed female. In older females, this neurological-bladder-sphincter control can begin to fail. For some unknown reason, the addition of female hormones, even though the amount of naturally circulating hormones is usually normal, seems to rejuvenate bladder control. Hormonal supplementation is very successful for this form of incontinence.

Bowel changes may occur due to the loss of muscle tone in the intestinal tract. The animal is considered constipated if the stool is of a hard consistency or the animal is painfully straining to pass it. Including increased amounts of fiber in the diet such as bran or vegetables can help. In recalcitrant cases, use of a stool softener such as Metamucil can alleviate the problem. Moderate use of vegetable oil may be included into the diet. Generally, if the pet does not pass a stool within a few days, fecal impaction should be suspected. This is a medical problem that should be immediately addressed. Enemas should only be administered under the instruction of the veterinarian.

Straining to eliminate stool may also be caused by an enlarged prostate in the older, uncastrated male. As the prostate increases in size, as it frequently and benignly does with age, it impinges on the lower intestinal tract. In some cases it can become an obstruction preventing the fecal matter from passing through in its normal manner. For this reason, any changes in the character of the bowel habit should be assessed by the practitioner immediately. Many practitioners are now encouraging a mid-life neutering of males in order to prevent prostate problems in their later years.

With either urine or stool incontinence, care should be taken to remove the urine or feces from the skin to prevent secondary dermatitis. If the animal has soiled himself, rinsing or shampooing of that particular area is all that is required. Careful drying, especially in colder weather, is imperative.

DENTAL CARE

In the past, little attention was paid to the dog's dental needs. Loss of teeth and gum disease were considered a normal part of the aging process. By the time the pet reached a truly antique age, it was expected that most, or all, of his teeth would have been lost. The newer approach is to provide routine tooth care throughout the animal's life by daily "brushing" and yearly dental examinations. A piece of gauze can be wrapped around the finger, covered with a small amount of C.E.T., a canine "toothpaste," and rubbed gently over the teeth and gums. This action will wear off any plaque before it has time to harden into a tenacious tartar.

For most elderly Shar-Pei, unused to having hands in their mouth, daily dental care is not well tolerated. In its absence, dry, crunchy food or chew toys will help to prevent the build up of tartar and plaque which undermines the dental structures.

Realistically, however, the front line of dental care will be provided by the veterinarian. He is able to remove the tartar build-up by use of a hand dental tool or an ultrasonic cleaner. Depending on the cooperation of the individual pet, this procedure may be able to be done without sedation or anesthesia. Should the dog not dutifully cooperate, as in any procedure requiring anesthesia for an elderly animal, the risks should be weighed against the benefits.

EXERCISE AND ENVIRONMENT

Moderation should typify the activity level of the older dog. While the dog is prone to arthritic changes of the joints, exercise should still be a part of the daily schedule. By encouraging movement, the muscles will maintain their tone, providing support to the joints.

Many older animals, given a choice, will elect to sleep. This inactivity accelerates the loss of muscle tone, the decrease in bone mass and a slow-down of all body systems. While energetic activity is equally harmful to arthritic joints, a leisurely stroll with the owner is highly beneficial.

If arthritis or joint degeneration is an ongoing condition, aspirin or other anti-inflammatory agents may be prescribed. (See Hip Dysplasia) Many pets with arthritis lead full and happy lives as long as the owner takes pains to minimize the environmental demands. If possible, the pet should be given access to the outdoors by way of as few stairs as possible. He should not be expected to trudge through deep snow to get to his "bathroom spot." Care should be taken to avoid icy sidewalks and slippery interior flooring. Jumping from car seat to ground, taken for granted for so many years, may be hazardous to the older pet. Just as the home and exterior were puppy-proofed when he joined the family, so the same should be done with the oldster's limitations in mind.

With age and more time spent sleeping, the prominent bony points of the hip, elbow and hock support an increased amount of the animal's weight. It is quite common for these areas to develop callouses from the constant pressure of flooring. Bedding should be thick and large enough that the dog can lie on his side and still be completely encompassed.

Extremes of temperature, either hot or cold, should be avoided. Older animals lack the ability to tolerate temperature fluctuations. Once merely an annoyance to the younger animal, it now can have a major impact on health. Physiologically perceived as a type of stress, it places excessive demands on the aging animal. Thus, year-round outdoor or unheated basement/garage kenneling is not suitable for the elderly Shar-Pei. Exercise during the summer months

Even this healthy horse coat Shar-Pei enjoys a sweater in the winter as he has very little undercoat to keep him warm. Bob Hope's Won Ton San of Shar-Pei Image Kennels.

should be provided in the early morning hours before the temperature and humidity climb.

BEHAVIOR

The old dog is by now a creature of habit. He is used to the pattern of family life. He enjoys the familiar, anticipates the usual, and basks in their security. With failing senses the older dog requires a consistent routine. Water and food bowls should be in the same spot, his mealtimes the same, his outings punctual. To introduce change is to remove the one element of stability upon which the geriatric dog depends.

If puppyhood can be seen as action in "fast-forward," adulthood as "normal" speed, old age is then "slow-motion." Decreased reflex time, body co-ordination and stamina all leave their impact on the old-timer's deportment. Elderly-proofing fragile home belongings is wise in view of the inevitable stumbles and bumps that failing eyesight and balance create.

At times it is possible for the aging to pet to become confused. He may suddenly become ''lost'' inside the house or cannot find his way through a half-opened door. Again, part of the aging process is the decline of mental abilities. Disciplining or scolding the dog will only serve to magnify his confusion and his insecurity. By gently and graciously leading the animal to his bed or other familiar location, the animal is allowed to maintain his dignity. If a state of confusion persists for more than an hour, veterinary assistance should be obtained.

TRAVELING

Changes in the pet's environment, once an exciting novel experience, are perceived as another stress placed on his fading coping abilities. While local car rides may still elicit an enthusiastic, puppyish response, traveling long distances or for long periods of time may adversely affect the pet. For most elderly, the comforts of a familiar bed, the same food, the known arrangement of furniture and predictable family routine all serve to support an animal whose senses are decreasing. In most cases, the kinder action may be to leave the pet at home with a loving and reliable caretaker.

Similarly, commercial kenneling of the geriatric dog is rarely successful. The total upheaval of food, environment and schedule places tremendous stresses on the pet. In some cases the stress may actually contribute to a physical decline in the dog's health. Many busy kennels are not able or willing to make the extra effort required for the aged pet. If kenneling is absolutely unavoidable, the owner should be sure that the kennel

Children and Shar-Pei are special. Le Ray's Wilbur of Ling Ling and his biggest fan, Heaven Smith.

has 24-hour attendant coverage and emergency veterinary care available. A list of approved boarding kennels can be obtained from the American Boarding Kennel Association, 4575 Galley Road, Suite 400-A, Colorado Springs, Colorado, 80915. The kennel and its individual enclosures should be personally inspected by the owner PRIOR to leaving the animal.

CHILDREN AND OTHER PETS

As the aging process advances, the personality of the pet may go through changes as well. The usually good-natured dog may become irritable or grouchy. This frequently comes as a surprise to owners who have taken his pleasant personality for granted. As the dog's infirmities begin to cause minor aches and pains, it naturally influences the dog's attitude. While regrettable, the animal should not be ostracized. As the home environment is changed to account for the physical limitations of the pet, so the family's expectations of the pet's moods should be in line.

Children, especially toddlers, present a difficult problem with the older pet. Unaware that they may be causing pain or discomfort to the animal by their over-zealous actions, the child must have adult intervention. Children should be supervised whenever playing with the animal. Crawling on, pulling at or physically harassing the animal should not be tolerated. Just as certain courtesies are taken when an elderly grandparent is present, so the child should behave respectfully towards the senior animal.

Other household pets may also be a problem area. While in the single-digit ages, a puppy may rejuvenate an older animal. The senior dog can act as a teacher of the younger animal and, frequently, will get obvious pleasure from its company. With animals that are quite elderly, however, a younger animal may be a source of physical and emotional stress. No longer able to truly participate in the activities, or desperately trying, the older dog may perceive the new addition as his replacement. Depression and withdrawal can occur.

VETERINARY CARE

As the pet's age advances, so the incidence of physical disorders will increase. The quality of the dog's years depends on their successful treatment. Many practitioners recommend that any animal that is ten years of age or older should be seen every six months. Lab tests may be done in order to monitor the dog's physical status. In this manner, developing medical conditions can be treated before they fulminate beyond the pet's ability to cope.

Signs of illness in the elderly pet that would indicate a need for immediate veterinary attention include the following:

- Sudden weight gain or loss
- Unexplained thirst
- Increased urinary output
- Muscular stiffness or difficulty rising or walking
- Urinary or bowel incontinence
- Coughing or shortness of breath
- Bad breath

It is inevitable that the ultimate condition of the pet will deteriorate to such a degree that the quality of life is no longer optimal. Sometimes Mother Nature takes the decision from the owner's shoulders but, more often, the owner must make the soul-wrenching decision whether medical care should continue.

MARILEE

A DOG'S PLEA

Treat me kindly, my beloved friend, for no heart in all the world is more grateful for kindness than the loving heart of me.

Do not break my spirit with a stick, for though I should lick your hand between blows, your patience and understanding will more quickly teach me the things you would have me learn.

Speak to me often, for your voice is the world's sweetest music, as you must know by the fierce wagging of my tail when your footstep falls on my waiting ear.

Please take me inside when it is cold and wet, for I am a domesticated animal, no longer accustomed to bitter elements. I ask no greater glory than the privilege of sitting at your feet beside the hearth.

Keep my pan filled with fresh water, for I cannot tell you when I suffer thirst.

Feed me clean food that I may stay well, to romp and play and do your bidding, to walk by your side, and stand ready, willing and able to protect you with my life, should your life be in danger.

And, my friend, when I am very old, and I no longer enjoy good health, hearing, and sight, do not make heroic efforts to keep me going . . . Please see that my trusting life is taken gently. I shall leave this earth knowing with the last breath I draw that my fate was always safest in your hands.

The Golden Dragon, a newsletter for Shar-Pei owners, reprinted this 1983 excerpt from an Ann Landers column. It is an eloquent statement of the final act of love.

GLOSSARY

Definitions from: Dorland's Illustrated Medical Dictionary, 25th edition, Philadelphia: W. B. Saunders, 1974.

abcess—a localized collection of pus in a cavity formed by the disintegration of tissues.

acute—having a short and relatively severe medical course.

abdomen—the portion of the body that lies between the thorax and the pelvis.

anemia—a reduction below normal in the number of red blood cells per cubic millimeter in the quantity of hemoglobin.

anorexia—lack or loss of the appetite for food.

antibody—an immunoglobulin molecule which interacts only with the antigen that induced its synthesis; classified according to their mode of action.

antigen—any substance which is capable of inducing the formation of antibodies and of reacting specifically in some detectable manner with the antibodies.

aspiration—the act of inhaling, especially vomitus.

axilla—the armpit; a small pyramidal space between the lateral chest and the medial side of the foreleg.

blepharospasm—squinting; tonic spasm of the orbicularis oculi muscle.

bradycardia—slowness of the heart's beating.

capillary—the minute vessels that connect the arterioles and venules of the circulatory system.

chronic—persisting over a long period of time.

congenital—existing at, and usually before, birth.

cornea—the transparent structure forming the anterior part of the fibrous tunic of the eye.

dorsal—pertaining to the back.

dyspnea—difficulty breathing.

edema—the presence of abnormally large amounts of fluid in the intercellular tissue spaces of the body.

electrolytes—a substance that dissociates into ions when fused or in solution; capable of conducting electricity in the body.

epithelium—the covering of internal and external surfaces of the body.

A pile of healthy Shar-Pei puppies. Yao'Shu's Blossom X Lynch's Playboy Ho Wun II. Margery Denton, photo.

excision—removal by cutting.

familial—occurring in or affecting more members of a family than would be expected by chance.

hereditary—genetically transmitted from parent to offspring.

hematoma—a localized collection of blood, usually clotted, due to a break in the wall of a blood vessel.

hypotension—abnormally low blood pressure; seen in shock but not necessarily indicative of it.

idiopathic—of unknown causation; peculiar to that individual.

immunity—the condition of being secure against the invasion or pathogenic effects of foreign microorganisms or to the toxic effect of antigenic substances.

incision—a cut, or a wound produced by cutting, with a sharp instrument.

infarct—an area of coagulation; tissue death due to lack of oxygen and nutrients resulting from obstruction of blood circulation to the area.

inguinal—pertaining to the groin; the junctional region between the abdomen and the thigh.

lesion—any pathological or traumatic discontinuity of tissue or loss of function of a part.

lumbar—pertaining to the loins; the part of the back between the thorax and the pelvis.

lymph node—any of the accumulations of lymphoid tissue organized as definite organs situated along the course of lymphoid vessels.

malignancy—a tendency to progress in virulence; used most frequently to refer to a cancerous state.

microfilariae—the prelarval stage of *Dirofilarial immitis* (heartworm) in the blood of dogs and in the tissues of mosquitoes.

neoplasm—any new and abnormal growth in which the growth is uncontrolled and progressive.

pruritus—itching.

pustules—a visible collection of pus within or beneath the epidermis.

pyoderma—any purulent skin disease.

stenosis—narrowing or stricture of a duct or canal.

systemic—pertaining to or affecting the body as a whole.

T-cells—T-lymphocytes; cells that are influenced by the thymus; responsible for cell-mediated immunity.

thorax—the part of the body between the neck and the respiratory diaphragm encased by the ribs; the chest.

topical—pertaining to a particular surface area.

vomitus—vomited matter.

The many faces of health. Yao'Shu's Cloisonne X Da Hei Xiong puppies. Margery Denton, photo.

BIBLIOGRAPHY

Dermatologic

Anderson, W. 1975. Canine Allergic Inhalant Dermatitis. Drum, S., editor. St. Louis: Ralston Purina Company.

Baker, E., V.M.D. 1987. Seborrhea: A Complex Complex. Veterinary Forum, April: 18-19.

Bussieras, J.; Chermette, R. 1986. Amitraz and Canine Demodicosis. Journal of the American Animal Hospital Association. Vol.22, Nov/Dec.: 779-782.

Campbell, K.L.; Vicini, D.S. 1985. Seborrhea. Dermatology Reports. Vol.4, No.3: 1-8.

Collins, J. 1981. My Favorite Remedy. The Orient Express, 25 February: 15.

Folz, S.D. 1983. Demodicosis (Demodex canis). Compendium on Continuing Education, Vol.5, No.2, February: 116-121.

Low, D.G., D.V.M. Personal Communication: Skin Disorders. University of California, 12 February 1987.

Mandelker, L., D.V.M. 1986. Allergic Dermatitis. Veterinary Forum, July: 14.

Muller, G.H., D.V.M. 1986. Skin Diseases of the Chinese Shar-Pei. The Barker, Nov/Dec.: 29-31.

Walter, J.B., M.D.; Israel, M.S., MRCPATH. 1978. General Pathology, 3rd ed. London: J & A Churchill: pp. 283-304.

Digestive

Batt, R.M. 1986. New Approaches to Malabsorption in Dogs. Compendium on Continuing Education, Vol.8, No.11, November: 783-792.

Davison, B., ed. 1983. Fact and Fiction on "Bloat." The Golden Dragon. Vol.2, No.2. April: 8-10.

————. 1984. Malabsorption Syndromes. The Golden Dragon, Vol.3, No.2. April: 11-14.

Fox, S.M., D.V.M. 1987. Crisis Management: Dealing with the Gastric Dilatation-Volvulus Syndrome. Veterinary Medicine, January: 36-58.

Giger, P., D.V.M. Personal Communication: Malabsorption. University of Pennslyvania, June 1987.

Jones, D., D.V.M., ed. 1986. Canine and Feline Gastroenterology. Philadelphia: W. B. Saunders Company: pp. 126-129, 168, 172-175, 188, 195-196.

Leib, M.S., D.V.M.; Blass, C.E., D.V.M. 1984. Acute Gastric Dilatation in the Dog: Various Clinical Presentations. Compendium on Continuing Education, Vol.6, No.8, August: 707-712.

————. 1984a. Gastric Dilatation-Volvulus in Dogs: An Update. Compendium on Continuing Education, Vol.6, No.11, November: 961-966.

Matthiesen, D.T., D.V.M. 1982. The Gastric Dilatation-Volvulus Complex: Medical and Surgical Considerations. Journal of the American Animal Hospital Association, Vol.19, Nov./Dec.: 925-932.

Muir, W.W., D.V.M.; Bonagura, J. D., D.V.M. 1984. Treatment of Cardiac Arrhythmias in Dogs with Gastric Distention-Volvulus. JAVMA, Vol.184, No.11, 1 June: 1366-1371.

Orton, C.E., D.V.M. 1986. Gastric Dilatation-Volvulus. Current Veterinary Therapy IX. Philadelphia: W. B. Saunders Company, pp. 856-857.

Schulman, A.J., D.V.M., et al. 1985. Muscular Flap Gastropexy: A New Surgical Technique to Prevent Recurrences of Gastric Dilation-Volvulus Syndrome. Journal of the American Animal Hospital Association, Vol.22, May/June: 339-346.

Ear, Nose and Throat

Ear

August, J.R. 1986. Evaluation of the Patient with Otitis Externa. Dermatology Reports. Vol.5, No. 2:1-3.

Bojrab, M.J., D.V.M., ed. 1983. External Ear. Current Techniques in Small Animal Surgery. Philadelphia: Lea & Febiger: pp. 96-99.

————. 1986a. Laying the Groundwork for Disease Management. Veterinary Medicine, July: 607-614.

————. 1986b. Otitis Externa: Seeing Past the Signs to Discover the Underlying Cause. Veterinary Medicine, July: 616-624.

Fox, S.M., D.V.M.; Woody, B.J., D.V.M. 1986. The Basics: Anatomy of the Canine Ear. Veterinary Medicine, July: 602-606.

Muller, G.H., D.V.M.; Kirk, R.W., D.V.M.; Scott, D.W., D.V.M. 1983. Ear Diseases. Animal Dermatology. 3rd ed. Philadelphia: W. B. Saunders Company: pp. 667-673.

Wilson, J.F. 1985. A Practitioner's Approach to Complete Ear Care. Dermatology Reports. Vol.4, No.2: 1-6.

Nose and Throat

Boudrieau, R.J., D.V.M. 1983. Megaesophagus in the Dog: A Review of 50 Cases. Journal of the American Animal Hospital Association, Vol.21, Jan./Feb.: 33-40.

Davison, B., ed. 1985. Addison's Disease Mimics Megaesophagus. The Golden Dragon, Vol.4, No.3. July: 5-7.

Ellison, G.W., D.V.M., et al. 1986. Esophageal Hiatal Hernia in Small Animals. Journal of the American Animal Hospital Association. Vol.23, July/August: 391-399.

Jones, B.D., D.V.M., ed. 1986. Canine and Feline Gastroenterology. Philadelphia: W. B. Saunders Company: pp. 62-79, 84-88, 157-160.

Spaulding, G.L., D.V.M., ed. 1985. Brachycephalic Airway Syndrome. The Veterinary Clinics of North America, Vol.15, No.5. Philadelphia: W. B. Saunders Company: pp. 903-909.

Endocrine

Baker, E., V.D.M. 1987. How Hypothyroidism Affects Dogs' Skin. Dog World. June: 12, 53-57.

Carlson, D.G., D.V.M.; Giffin, J.M., M.D. 1984. Dog Owner's Home Veterinary Handbook. New York: Howell Book House, Inc.: pp. 41-2, 83-5.

Davison, B., ed. 1985. Further Comments on Addison's Disease. The Golden Dragon. Vol.4, No.4. October: 5.

Degen, M.A.. D.V.M.; Breitschwerdt, E.B., D.V.M. 1986. Canine and Feline Immunodeficiency, Part I. Compendium on Continuing Education, Vol.8, No.6, June: 641-648.

Dhein, C.R., D.V.M. Personal Communication: immunodeficiency. Washington State University. February, 1987.

Fraser, C.M., ed. 1986. The Merck Veterinary Manual. 6th ed. Rahway, New Jersey: Merck & Company, Inc.: pp. 254-269.

Giger, P., D.V.M. Personal Communication: immunodeficiency. Genetics Dept., University of Pennslyvania. July, 1987.

Guilford, W.G. 1987. Primary Immunodeficiency Diseases in Dogs and Cats. Compendium Small Animal, Vol.9, No.6, June: 641-648.

Moroff, S.D., et al. 1986. IgA Deficiency in Shar-Pei Dogs. Veterinary Immunology and Immunopathology, Vol.13. Amsterdam: Elsevier Science Publishers B.V.: pp. 181-188.

Nelson, R.W.; Ihle, S.L., D.V.M. 1987. Hypothyroidism in Dogs and Cats: A Difficult Deficiency to Diagnose. Veterinary Medicine. January: 60-70.

Walter, J.B., M.D.; Israel, M.S., MRCPATH. 1978. Immunological Mechanism. General Pathology. 3rd ed. London: J & A Churchill: pp. 47-70, 259-261.

Geriatric

Care and Feeding of the Older Dog. 1980. Los Angeles: Carnation Company.

Caring for the Older Dog. 1986. Tarrytown, New York: Gaines Foods, Inc.: 2-14.

Carlson, D.G., D.V.M.; Giffin, J.M., M.D. 1984. Dog Owner's Home Veterinary Handbook. New York: Howell Book House, Inc.: pp. 335-340.

Garvey, M.S., et al. "Canine Geriatrics." Symposium at the Eastern States University Conference. Alpo Pet Center, Pennsylvania. January, 1986: 12-20.

Hall, J. 1984. Caring for the Older Dog. Knoxville: Ralston Purina Company.

Health Parameters

Anderson, M.; Beane, C. 1987. Heartworm Prevention. Dog Fancy, March: 54-56.

Carlson, D.G., D.V.M.; Giffin, J.M., M.D. 1984. Dog Owner's Home Veterinary Handbook. New York: Howell Book House, Inc.: pp. 209-213.

Dogs, Cats, and Roundworms. 1986. Veterinary Medicine (Supplement), August: 1-5.

Fraser, C.M., ed. 1986. The Merck Veterinary Manual. 6th ed. Rahway, New Jersey: Merck & Company, Inc.: pp. 67-9, 903-14.

MSDAGVET. Heartguard Informational pamphlet. Division of Merck & Company, Inc. Rahway, New Jersey.

Infertility

Davison, B., ed. 1984. Canine Brucellosis. The Golden Dragon. Vol.3, No.1. Jan.: 4-8.

Johnston, S.D., D.V.M.; Rakel, S., D.V.M. 1987. Fetal Loss in the Dog and Cat. The Veterinary Clinics of North America. Vol.17, No.3, May: 535-564.

Olson, P.N.; Behrendt, M.D.; Weiss, D.E. 1987. Reproductive Problems in the Bitch: Formulating Your Diagnostic Plan. Veterinary Medicine. May: 482-494.

Umstead, J.A., V.M.D. 1986. Infertility in the Male Dog and Cat. Kal Kan Forum. Vol.5, No.3, Summer: 4-10.

Opthalmic

Bachrach, G. Personal Communication: Entropion. Veterinary Opthalmology of New England, May 1987.

Bojrab, M.J., D.V.M.; Crane, S.W., D.V.M.; Arnoczky, S.P., D.V.M. 1983. Current Techniques in Small Animal Surgery. Philadelphia: Lea & Febiger: 30-34.

Davidson, M.G., D.V.M.; Nasisse, M.D., D.V.M. 1986. Ocular Diseases of the Young Dog and Cat. Kal Kan Forum. Winter: 4-5.

Donovan, R. Personal Communication: Eye Surgery. Boston, May 1987.

"Entropion." Veterinary Surgical Forum, American College of Veterinary Ophthalmologist. Chicago, 1983.

Holmberg, D.L. 1980. Temporary Correction of Entropion in the Young Dog. Modern Veterinary Practice. Vol.61, No.4: 345-346.

Holt, J.R. 1984. Cautery for Entropion. Veterinary Record. Vol.115, No.1: 22-23.

Kuhns, E.L., D.V.M. 1982. Repair of Congenital Bilateral Entropion in the Dog. Veterinary Medicine. August: 1198-1201.

Lenarduzzi, R.F. 1983. Management of Eyelid Problems in Chinese Shar-Pei Puppies. Veterinary Medicine, April: 548-550.

McKibben, J.S. 1981. The Rare Shar-Pei Dog: Medical and Surgical Problems. Veterinary Medicine. Vol.76: 997-1002.

Roberts, S.M., D.V.M. Personal Communication: Eye Disease. Colorado State University, College of Veterinary Medicine, February 1987.

Severin, G.A., D.V.M. 1976. Veterinary Ophthalmology Notes. 2nd ed. Colorado: Colorado State University: 94-97.

Slatter, D.H. 1981. Nictitating Membrane. Fundamentals of Veterinary Ophthalmology. Philadelphia: W.B.Saunders Company: pp. 216-225, 311-317, 625.

Quinn, A.J., D.V.M. Personal Communication: Eye Disease in the Shar-Pei. American Society of Veterinary Opthalmology, February 1987.

Orthopedic

Alexander, J.W., D.V.M.; Earley, T.D., D.V.M. 1984. A Carpal Laxity Syndrome in Young Dogs. Journal of Veterinary Orthopedics. Vol.3, No.1: 22-26.

Beu, J., radiologist. Personal Communication: bowed forelegs. Mississippi State University. May, 1987.

Bojrab, M.J., D.V.M.; Crane, S.N., D.V.M. 1983. Patellar Surgery. Current Techniques in Small Animal Surgery. Philadelphia: Lea & Febiger: pp. 650-653.

LaCroix, J.A., D.V.M. 1980. Patella Luxation. American Kennel Gazette. October: 74.

Lau. R.E., D.V.M. 1977. Inherited Premature Closure of Distal Ulnarphysis. Journal of American Animal Hospital Association. Vol.13: 609-612.

—————. Personal Communication: Premature closure of long bone growth plates. June 1987.

McKibben, J.S., D.V.M. 1981. The Rare Shar-Pei Dog: Medical and Surgical Problems. Veterinary Medicine. July: 997-1002.

Wilson, T., D.V.M. Personal Communication: Bowed Forelegs. Airport Road Hospital, Memphis, Tenn. June 1987.

Dental

Bath, S. 1986. Fat Lip Surgery in the Meat-Mouth Chinese SharPei. The Golden Dragon. Vol.4, No.1. January: 11-14.

Brannan, R., D.V.M. Personal Communication: Dentistry in the Shar-Pei. Mawnee, Ohio. 1987.

Clarke, E. 1987. Shar-Pei Health. Dog World. April: 146-148.

Grove, K.T., V.M.D. 1986. Interceptive Orthodontics. Veterinary Forum. April: 15.

—————. 1986a. Oral Surgery. Veterinary Forum. June: 9.

Tamke, P.G., V.M.D. 1986. Dentistry in Dogs and Cats. Kal Kan Forum. Vol.5, No.3, Summer: 11-17.

Hip Dysplasia

Anonymous. Canine Hip Dysplasia. Orthopedic Foundation for Animals informational sheet.

Artificial Joints Supplement Nature. 1986. DVM. December: 36.

Carlson, D.G., D.V.M.; Giffin, J.M., M.D. 1984. Dog Owner's Home Veterinary Handbook. New York: Howell Book House, Inc.: pp. 233-235.

Clarke, A.P., D.V.M. 1984. Canine Clinic. New York: MacMillan Publishing Company: pp. 214-217.

Davison, B., ed. 1982. Hip Dysplasia. The Golden Dragon. Vol.1, No.3. July: 9-13.

Fitzpatrick, T. Personal Communication: X-raying for Dysplasia. Vet Care Clinic, Albuquerque, N.M. June 1987.

Fraser, C.M., ed. 1986. The Merck Veterinary Manual. 6th ed. Rahway, New Jersey: Merck & Company, Inc.: pp. 460-461.

Kealy, R.D., PhD.; Lawler, D.F., D.V.M.; Reutzel, L.F., PhD. 1985. Ralston Purina Research on Canine Hip Dysplasia. Ralston Purina Company.

Lanting, F.; Riser, W.H.; Olsson, S. 1981. Canine Hip Dysplasia. Loveland, Colorado: Alpine Publications, Inc.

Wease, G.N., D.V.M.; Corley, E.A., D.V.M. 1985. Howell, L.D., ed. Control of Canine Hip Dysplasia: Current Status. Kal Kan Forum. Vol.4, No.4. Fall: 80-88.

Yuk Lan at her post as Look-out. June Collins, owner /breeder.

GENERAL INDEX

Note the heavy wrinkling of these eight week old pups. Helen Armacost, breeder.

A profile of the Shar-Pei's "hippopotamus" head. LeRay's Wilbur of Ling Ling at 10 months. Theresa Morgan, owner.

Kim Wah's Bee Bee Niche at eleven weeks. Kasu Kennels.

Daisy Hills Andante, age three-four months. Nancy Mellema, owner.

Ch. Tai-Pan's Odie of Kasu, C.D. "Odie." Kasu Kennels.

Lucky Wun's Cinderella and Lucky Wun's Prince Charming. Rosie Steinke, owner.